D1624535

BLIND
FURY

BLIND FURY

ANNA FLOWERS

PINNACLE BOOKS
WINDSOR PUBLISHING CORP.

PINNACLE BOOKS are published by

Windsor Publishing Corp.
475 Park Avenue South
New York, NY 10016

Pinnacle and the P logo are trademarks of Windsor
Publishing Corp.

Printed in the United States of America

ISBN 1-55817-719-1

Dedicated with love to Belle and David.

This book was written using public records produced in court during Gerald Stano's numerous criminal cases. Whenever possible, actual events have been recreated with minimal fictionalization. The names of the principal parties are real; the only name which has been changed is Eddie Mann.

Thanks to the many people of central Florida who assisted me in the preparation of this book. Special thanks to my agents at Writer's Edge, Dana Pomeroy and Al Link. Thanks also to the Volusia and Brevard County Sheriff's Departments, and of course, Paul Crow, who graciously agreed to write the foreword and who is unquestionably the hero of this book.

should have signaled the beginning of the end of hundreds of hours of exhaustive and sometimes frustrating efforts by several jurisdictions, it was only the beginning. This investigation ultimately became a test of the very strength that philosophically binds the criminal justice system together. Above all, it became a test of willpower . . . the resolution of a diabolical and homicidal personality against a career-oriented police investigator.

In retrospect, it seems almost inconceivable that an investigation, so significant in its consequences, and so devastating in its effect on the lives of so many ordinary Floridians, could encounter so many obstacles. Just for a moment, imagine a system where there is no statewide prosecution system, allowing each judicial circuit to investigate differently, regardless of resources to do so. Also, imagine a wide disparity in knowledge about serial murders or psychological profiles and their uses in these cases, lack of knowledge about interview techniques, personality conflicts among investigators, inadequate and incomplete crime scene investigations, and shallow, unrevealing postmortem examinations. In some instances, there was a lack of support from a chief law enforcement administrator to pursue investigative leads with the diligence these cases warranted. Above all, a concise and comprehensive media policy designed to inform the public and warn potential suspects was virtually nonexistent. If you can imagine an investigative environment such as this, you must vicariously sense my frustrations in attempting to bring this Gerald Eugene Stano to justice.

When information first surfaced indicating the possible scope of this investigation which would include multiple law enforcement agencies, state attorneys offices, medical examiners, crime scene investigations, and witnesses, the obstacles seemed insurmountable. Because of the complexity and disjointedness of the system, it was very possible for anyone as diabolical as Gerald Stano to slip through.

Initial contacts with investigators working related unsolved homicides often indicated a total lack of understanding about serial murders. Many of these investigators were either indifferent or refused to accept psychological profiling as an investigative tool. Overall, there was a general lack of interest or ability to see through the "mind's eye" of the person on whom the investigation was focused.

As interest in this case began to grow, several other challenges began to surface, most prominently, the personalities of the investigators and the idiosyncrasies of their various jurisdictions. Because of the publicity this case began to receive, there was a scrambling, almost a race, to see who could outdo who, without consideration for, or coordination with, agencies investigating related cases. These "ego" challenges led to duplication of efforts and frustrations for everyone involved.

From a technical perspective, crime scene investigations and postmortem examinations presented major challenges. Many jurisdictions lacked effective crime scene policy, therefore, in many of the jurisdictions involved, very little emphasis was placed on protecting a crime scene from contamination. Valuable evidence was often either overlooked or destroyed. Furthermore, many crime scene investigators lacked the knowledge and technical expertise in these types of crimes to comprehensively process the scenes. In addition, forensic pathology received neither the attention nor funding necessary to adequately determine conclusive evidentiary priorities.

The most challenging obstacle was the lack of knowledge or training and the differences in attitudes on the part of investigators to successfully perform an interview and/or interrogation. Weaknesses in this basic investigative area led to exaggerated fears and hesitation on the part of many investigators from the various jurisdictions involved in these cases. Many times, information that could have been obtained, without the compromise of individual constitutional rights, was not obtained because of a lack of understanding of constitutional law. The time involved in this investigation would have been considerably shorter if investigators had been better trained and more familiar with constitutional law.

Another very important challenge presented during this investigation was the scope and impact of the media on our efforts and effects on families and friends of victims. During this period, very few, if any, of the law enforcement agencies involved had a comprehensive media relations policy. Because of the newsworthiness of facts surrounding this case, information concerning the victims, the crime scene, and other valuable information was released to the public prematurely. The consequences were devastating to those who might be termed "secondary victims": family, relatives and friends. The situation also did little to help the overall investigative efforts as well.

Even in the shadow of these obstacles, Gerald Stano confessed to the murder of forty-two women. For his acts, this convicted killer received eight life sentences and three death sentences.

Today, many of the obstacles I encountered in the Gerald Stano investigation no longer exist in the state of Florida. Modern criminal investigation has taken on a whole new meaning, especially when applied to serial crimes, particularly murders. However, other obstacles have created a brick wall for the administration of justice. Since

1982, Stano's execution has been stalled time and time again. It is important for me to note here that I believe in the appeals process; however, the current appeals system needs to be overhauled to prevent excessive tax dollars and time being spent to "run around in circles" time and time again over the same appeal issues. It is my opinion, for instance, that written affidavits should be replaced by personal testimony before the circuit judge, where possible, to determine their validity before appellate issues are referred to the appeals court. Furthermore, I believe that all appeals should be exhausted prior to the issuance of a death warrant.

Justice is delicate—a proper balance between an individual suspect's constitutional rights and the individual victim's constitutional rights makes it so. Many questions arise when pondering individual rights. We cannot live in a perfect society with perfect laws and a perfect justice system. That should not stop us, however, from constantly striving to improve the system and maintain the balance that justice demands.

Our justice system also deserves more attention and resources to help improve its performances. Ideally, we will one day learn to prevent acts of criminal violence insofar as possible. We must recognize that there is a connection between the economic, social, and psychological problems of society and crime. The need will always exist for training in the new and innovative techniques mentioned earlier to expedite investigations. Jurisdictional cooperation is necessary in the very mobile society in which we live. Up-to-date policies on evidence/crime procedures and media announcements are beginning to emerge as the criminal justice system moves into the future. While I experienced years of frustration with this particular case, I am encouraged by strides made since this investigation began and by new trends I see emerging in state-of-the-art criminal investigation as well as for society's interest in the administration of justice.

PAUL B. CROW
Director of Public Safety
Daytona Beach, Florida

Prologue

In the 1930s when the boardwalk was first built, the coquina shell open-air auditorium was the focal point of social life in Daytona Beach, Florida. Well-dressed families in white suits and straw hats gathered at the bandshell to enjoy band music by the sea. In the evening, in their finery, they would stroll down the boardwalk visiting friends, inhaling salt air and eating saltwater taffy, trying to look prosperous. Not so active folks sat in wicker rockers on hotel porches and critiqued the passersby. A crackling radio might tell you whether John Rockefeller was at his winter home in Ormond Beach.

The combination of fast cars and firm sand was the original tourist attraction. Racing pioneers Alexander Winston and Ransom Olds gave Daytona its reputation as the world center of speed near the turn of the century when they began racing their horseless carriages on the white sand. Racing on the beach reached a frenzy in the thirties when Sir Malcolm Campbell posted a run of over 330 miles per hour in his Bluebird. Later, faster cars, larger crowds and increased beach development caused the stock car races to move to Daytona International Speedway.

In the 1970s when Gerald Eugene Stano arrived, Daytona was no longer an elegant hostess extending southern hospitality. Stano was drawn to the beachside's malignant heart. Ocean Avenue formed a loop with Highway A1A where tough, overcrowded bars blared music, amusement centers highlighted video games, and bumper-to-bumper cars droned along the beach. At twenty-two years old, he found the area fascinating. Degenerates congregated in front of run-down rooming houses. Prostitutes beckoned from the porches where the affluent once rocked in their wicker chairs. Runaways flocked to this seamy side of Daytona Beach. It was from these players that he chose most of his victims.

During his grisly seven-year killing spree, Stano confessed he murdered forty-two women, making him one of the most prolific serial killers of this century.

One

January 27, 1980

The sun dipped below the Halifax River as Gerald Stano merged his car into the stream of eastbound traffic heading for the ocean at Daytona Beach. Winter was his favorite time of year because it got dark early.

At the stoplight he removed his dark glasses and rubbed his eyes. He ran his fingers through his receding black hair. *At least it's not grey,* he thought looking in the rearview mirror. *I need a beer,* he decided.

When the light changed, he pulled into a convenience store. Beer was the last thing his fleshy body needed. At five foot nine, he weighed nearly two hundred pounds. Roller skating kept his legs in shape but it was his only form of exercise. Now that he was approaching thirty, his beer belly had begun to poke over his belt. Jerry had always been sensitive about his weight and to compensate, his appearance was usually meticulously neat. He had enjoyed disco dancing but it was fading. Still afflicted with Saturday night fever, however, his idea of "fashionable" was a printed polyester shirt open at the neck. He also wore a black and gold high school ring. He bought himself a six-pack of beer and another pack of cigarettes.

Jerry blinked his eyes in nervous habit and carefully counted his change. When this money was gone, he would be flat broke again. Unemployment was a reoccurring problem for him. He left his last job as a Canada Dry deliveryman without notice two weeks ago. For four months he had made more money than ever, but he was tired of selling soda. Before Canada Dry, there was the job with Zeno Marine for four months working as an apprentice mechanic. His boss liked him, and had called him a gentleman. Jerry wondered if he should not have stayed at Zeno. He liked the food service jobs better than the mechanic jobs. The "Cook Wanted" sign at Hampton's Restaurant had caught his attention earlier. Maybe he'd check into that tomorrow. Actually, some of Stano's employers had kind words to say about him. He left without notice or broke a few rules, but generally he was a good worker. He blended into the background, the faceless guy who cooked your burger or pumped your gas.

Few people saw his other face and lived to tell about it.

Orange Avenue took Stano to Memorial Bridge

which spanned the Halifax River, connecting the mainland and the beachside peninsula. The new courthouse annex on City Island in the river stood guard at the west end of the bridge. The three-story modern structure with tall columns cast an imposing shadow at twilight. Jerry paid little attention to it.

The traffic was heavy for a Sunday night, he decided as he headed to the beachside. The Daytona 500 race was still two weeks away but the races leading up to it started in a few days. Stock car racing's only million-dollar purse for the 500 was a powerful drawing card. It was the first major race of the season, and the excitement was accelerated. Race fans were already converging on Daytona Beach to watch practice sessions at the famous 2.5-mile tri-oval track on the west side of town. Add to the race fans the usual flock of snowbirds fleeing the harsh northern winter and the town filled up fast.

"Damn tourists. Don't you know where you're going?" he shouted. He hit the brakes and swerved into the next lane to avoid a car full of pointing sightseers. *That was too close for comfort,* he thought and flipped them the bird as he passed.

Daytona Beach residents prepare for waves of tourists every spring. In early February, the NAS-CAR-sponsored events at the International Speedway bring several hundred thousand race fans into a town of fifty thousand. Huge campers bearing license plates from all over North America rumble around and gather in parking lots. Race fans from every town and hollow buy new red jackets emblazoned with their favorite brand of cigarettes or beer, jump in their Monte Carlos and head south. Older and generally a well behaved lot, the only negative by-product of this first group of the year is the traffic. Every driver thinks he's the next Bill Elliot. They weave and dart through the tangled traffic that chokes usually drowsy residential streets.

No sooner has the last race team packed up and a collective sigh of relief is expelled when a faint rumble begins. The thunderous roar grows to a deafening climax as motorcycles swarm into town for Bike Week. The American Motorcyclist Association sponsors the Daytona 200 and Supercross races in early March. It seems every Harley-Davidson ever made can be found on Main Street. Black leather is the clothing choice. Tattoos are proudly displayed on every conceivable part of the human anatomy. Some people create body murals. Earrings pierce nipples and noses. Long grey manes and beards flow from helmets as all age groups are represented. It seems like Halloween where all come costumed as Hell's Angels. Motorcycle Mamas hanging on the back of hogs are a breed all their own. Knowing some women will oblige suggestions to "Show us your tits," schoolboys flock to Main Street hoping to get lucky.

In the 1970s, Bike Week was heralded by massive arrests and general hostility by the city fathers. The parade of motorcycles, a favorite event of bikers, had been threatened with extinction. Over the years the mood has changed. Beginning in 1989, Daytona Beach Police Chief Paul Crow mounted a chopper to lead the biker's parade.

Late March also brings an annual invasion of college students and other young party seekers to Datona's warm beaches. Connie Francis told college girls where the boys were in the early sixties, and she meant Fort Lauderdale. That south Florida city was the Spring Break capital for many years. Then in 1961, a crackdown by officials sent many collegians north to Daytona Beach. When Stano made the scene, thousands of young people and students came during the rite of spring. The atmosphere is "enjoy," and law enforcement consists primarily of quelling rowdy parties. Although bike and race weeks bring many of the same people back each year, Spring Break brings new hedonists every season.

Beginning in the mid 1970s, Spring Break activities changed. Concerts at the bandshell drew thousands along the boardwalk. Live radio shows later gave way to MTV broadcasts from beach hotels. The "College Expo '76" brought nearly one hundred companies and has grown every year since then. Tents sprung up along the beach where promoters gave away samples, T-shirts, and posters advertising their products. So many students from all over the country descend on Daytona that companies started test marketing to capture a national sample.

Students were interested in free merchandise, but the real attraction was other young people, the sun, and the sand. All of this was accessible by car. Spring breakers, along with race fans and bikers, created a strange, freewheeling atmosphere. Everyone arrived in town ready for parties and wild times. Motels, bars, souvenir shops, and game parlors accommodated party animals. Like many other locals, Stano worked in businesses dependent on the lucrative tourist trade. Living and working in a tourist town was exciting for Jerry since the festive vacation atmosphere was intoxicating.

Stano drove the few blocks across the thin peninsula. He turned north on A1A, the busy honky-tonk highway that runs parallel with the ocean. Stano knew this strip better than most because he spent hours here cruising by neon light. He often bragged that he could name every motel in order.

Stano crushed out his cigarette and popped another beer. He drove down onto the beach. What had intrigued him most about Daytona Beach when he first visited his grandparents here was the social side of the beach scene. In the northeast, "beach" meant a sea of bodies strewn on a sliver of sand. At Daytona, the twenty-three miles of wide, sandy beach along the Atlantic Ocean was completely different. Here the gentle slope allowed the incoming tide to pack the sand so firmly that it could support automobiles. Cars are an integral part of beach life, providing music and an instant party kit. Cars, crawling along at the ten-mile-per-hour speed limit, become an extension of the individual. To see and be seen is the purpose of the motorized parade that snakes for miles. Guys troll along the beach watching girls saunter by. Casual conversations between scantily clad beachgoers quickly lead to friendships. Often strollers jump into a car for a ride up the beach. Stano had always been preoccupied with cars but found making friends difficult. He was mesmerized by all the new fish available in his sea and this new method of hooking them.

This evening, as he had done so many times before, Stano parked his car on the beach and watched the waves roll in, drinking beer and smoking cigarettes. He heard laughter in the next car, disturbing his reverie. Looking over, he saw a young couple embracing. He quickly looked away, embarrassed and envious. "Get a room," he snorted. The reminder of his own inadequacy was maddening. He just could not understand why he never had good relationships with women.

After all, I'm a good looking guy, he mused. *A real Italian stallion. If I had someone right now I'd take her disco dancing, or maybe I'd just ride her around listening to music. I'm a real gentleman.* His face clouded. *It's all their fault. They always make me angry: bitching, criticizing my car or my clothes. Or worst of all, flirting like a whore, teasing me and then turning me down. Bitch, bitch,*

bitch. I have to kill them just to shut them up.
Then he thought of his wife. *Another real bitch,* he
concluded.

Thinking of his pathetic ex-wife made him even
more sullen. *She's the one who couldn't do anything right, not even fuck. It's all her fault that I'm
looking for a piece of ass right now.* To convince
himself, he said aloud, "She's the one with the
problem." He winced at the image of her. *Even the
shrink said she was a compulsive eater.* He collected stray ashes from the seat cover and wiped
them on a tissue. He drained his beer. He opened
yet another bêer and lit another cigarette. Mickey
had despised his chain-smoking.

He thought about their wedding in June, 1975,
and the honeymoon at Pompano Beach. *If I had
known the honeymoon would be the last time
Mickey wanted sex, I would have skipped Disney
World,* he thought. He mellowed a little and realized that they really didn't have a very good start.
Maybe if they had lived somewhere other than in
that small trailer she would have liked it better.
Maybe if her mother and sister hadn't hung around
all the time he would have stayed home more. He
hated working for her father at the Shell station.
Maybe he shouldn't have shot her horse or choked
her poodle, but he had hated that damn zoo of
hers. *Hard to believe that lousy marriage lasted
over a year!*

"The Jerry you people know is different from the

24

Jerry who lives with me." He still couldn't believe Mickey had written that to his parents. Rage welled in him. He felt under his seat by the door and fingered his knife. The moment passed, and he regained control of himself. This was the beginning of a new year, a new decade. He vowed to quit while he was ahead. He would stop killing women before he was caught. The world would never know the other Jerry, the brutal Jerry. For him, the urge for sex was confused with the lust to kill. Yet, he knew that he would eventually be caught if he continued. He must stop now. His life depended on it.

He crushed the beer can and tossed it in a plastic bag. Stano would not allow a single drop of beer to soil his car. He loved his car in a way he had never loved a person. Jerry referred to the highlights of his life by remembering the car he drove at the time. His current passion was a shiny red 1977 AMC Gremlin, a two-door model with tinted windows and a front tag that read, "No riders except brunettes, blondes or redheads." Stano was proud of the stereo, which was particularly loud. The car had lots of heavy chrome on the luggage rack and bumpers, and there was no evidence of rust or salt spray damage because he washed it every day.

Stano enjoyed long car trips. He would drive a thousand miles just to see how long it took him. In 1973, he drove from Pennsylvania to Gainesville, Florida; murdered two young girls; and then drove immediately back home to Pennsylvania. As a Florida resident a few years later, he often drove to cities and towns a hundred miles away to kill or dispose of bodies. Many of his victims were selected from and laid to rest along Florida's major interstate highways: I-4, I-75, and I-95.

The last beer was history, and Stano decided it was time to get rolling again. He headed north up the beach. He drove slowly under the pier, and he could faintly hear the music from the dance hall drifting in with the tide. Sometimes he liked to dance here above the sea, but not tonight. At Main Street he drove up the beach ramp and saw a noisy, rowdy crowd in the Red Garter topless bar on the corner. Despite the hordes of visitors, Stano could still easily spot the prostitutes.

Automatically, Stano headed north on Ocean Avenue, and circled like a shark around the seven-block loop made by Ocean and Atlantic Avenues.

Maybe I should call it a night and go home, he thought half-heartedly, but he knew he would not spend his evening in front of the tube in his one-room efficiency apartment at the Riviera Hotel. It was one of a string of dismal rooms that Jerry had rented along Ridgewood Avenue. The only decent houses he had ever lived in were owned by his father.

Turning south on A1A, Stano saw more T-shirt shops, hash houses, and topless bars. He passed Main Street again and noticed a police car in front of the Red Garter. They really were rowdy tonight. At the south end of the Loop, he turned north again on Ocean Avenue. Two drunk college girls stumbled out of the Ocean Deck bar.

"Need a ride?" he asked.

"No thanks," they laughed and staggered away.

Their ebbing voices grated on his nerves. His anger and frustration intensified.

After a couple more passes around the loop, he selected a working girl and rolled down his tinted window to make a pitch.

"Want to party?" he asked, forcing his voice to sound amiable.

"Sure thing, honey," she smiled. She turned and walked to the wall surrounding the bandshell. Huddling with another hooker, she glanced anxiously back toward him. She grabbed the other woman's arm for fortification and shouted at him.

"Get lost man. I know who you are." Her eyes flashed frightened and angry. "I don't want the shit beat out of me. Fuck off." Both women hurried away.

The tires squealed when he took off. He stabbed his fingers into the cigarette pack and fished out the last one. *The nerve of that whore,* he thought, crushing the empty pack. He passed the Holiday Inn again. A blonde hitchhiker in tight jeans caught his eye. He screeched to a stop and opened the door.

"Want a ride?" He managed a smile.

Her response was to slip into the seat next to him. The red Gremlin disappeared into the night.

Two

January-February 1980

Mary Carol Maher was a tall, good-looking college girl who was training for a future in swimming competition. She was already a champion in high school and college, but this was expected of her since both her sister and brother were competitive swimmers. The conflict was that Mary Carol had an outgoing personality and healthy good looks that were distracting. Training was becoming boring. The athletic ability came naturally, but not the discipline necessary to sustain a serious swimming career.

Her mother understood this and was Mary Carol's strongest supporter. She gave her daughter breathing space even though she still lived at home, straining her mother's second marriage. She knew that her vivacious daughter had potential, but directing Mary Carol's boundless energy was difficult.

Mary Carol liked Daytona's nightlife and went dancing two or three times a week. Going out was

28

the only fun she allowed in her busy schedule of training, attending classes at the community college, and working at a restaurant. She had many friends in Daytona Beach. Mary Carol could walk into one of her favorite hangouts, like Fanny Farkel's or the bar at Holiday Inn Boardwalk, and always see several familiar faces. Although many of her high school buddies had gone on to college, some had stayed in town to work or attend the local colleges. This core of friends was one of the few pleasures in her life at the moment. She enjoyed partying with them and sometimes stayed out all night, but she always called home. Lack of mobility was her biggest social problem. If her mother didn't drive her, she had to get rides from friends. Often she preferred to hitchhike.

She had made a New Year's resolution to try to get her life more organized. Here it was the end of January and she had been unable to make any significant improvement. It had been almost two years since she graduated from Mainland High School. She missed the total confidence that teenagers possess. In high school, choices seemed easier and more clear-cut. She had joined the Future Secretaries Club and had a steady boyfriend. Her future seemed secure but mundane. True to her tempestuous nature, Mary Carol backed out. She just couldn't face a life of typing and housework. She was determined not to pattern her life after her mother's.

Her mom endured a stifling second marriage, which was now on the rocks. She felt a twinge of guilt realizing that she was responsible for some of the misunderstanding between her mother and stepfather. But Mary Carol was not about to let anyone tell her how to live. She had decided to try to get somewhere in life through swimming. She took classes to keep her mother happy, and she worked as a waitress for spending money. Her energy ebbed under such tremendous demands.

She found herself at a crossroad and had to make some difficult choices. Her last relationship had ended when she refused to have a baby. Mary Carol thought about her former boyfriend now as she did her warm-up exercises poolside. He had simply been too much to resist: a six foot tall, dark and handsome Latin lover. She thought of his curly black hair and wide smile. She had admired his well-conditioned body, but had never really loved him. There was no room in her life right now for a lasting relationship, and certainly not for a baby. She had done the right thing, she convinced herself, and he was definitely ancient history.

"No hard feelings," he had said as they made the parting official. "You're a great girl, Mary Carol, and I won't forget you."

"I can forget you," she exclaimed to no one in particular. Mary Carol stuffed her hair under her cap and fully extended her one hundred twenty pounds into a well executed dive. It was good to feel the water and to have the pool to herself. There was seldom anyone else here this early in the morning, and she liked that. A few more laps and she would dry off and go to work.

She changed into the Hawaiian print shirt and shorts that were her work uniform. Bahama Joe's Restaurant was not a bad place to work. The people there were nice and the slate floors helped condition her legs. The lunch crowd usually tipped generously. Friendly locals liked the seafood specials and reduced prices for drinks around noontime, but today's crowd was uncharacteristically unpleasant and reinforced her resolve to quit. The notoriously slow kitchen was worse than usual because the new cook barely spoke English. Mary Carol screamed at him as if volume could overcome the language barrier. After that he made sure her orders were last. Her customers grew surly, and her tips shrank drastically. Ending the tiresome shift, she dropped a tray of glasses that cost her a significant portion of her pay.

As she opened the front door, she heard loud, angry voices and then her mother's bedroom door slammed shut. Her stepfather came out and wanted to continue the argument with her. *The hell with you,* she thought.

"I don't need this," she hissed and slipped past him down the hall. Her green eyes burned with hatred.

Later that night after complaining long-distance

to her real father, Mary Carol asked her mother to drive her to the disco lounge at the Holiday Inn. It was ten thirty and Mary Carol had decided to try to improve what was left of her evening.

As she walked into the disco, Mary Carol looked much better than she felt. She had her long blond hair in a ponytail pulled to the side and wore a long-sleeved black silk shirt. The blouse had an interesting design of a monkey on a zebra's back. The rest of her looked great, too, in tight blue jeans wrapped around a trim behind and long legs. A shoulder purse swung against her hip as she made her entrance. When she climbed into a seat at the bar, the bartender, an old friend, stepped into the flack of her bad mood.

He was surprised to find her so argumentative. He tried the usual light conversation, but that didn't work.

"This drink is water," she snapped. "You got a new scam going on here? How about putting some booze in this." She pushed the drink across the bar and it splashed the front of his shirt. "Hey, I'm sorry," she said contritely and lowered her head into her hands. His anger turned to sympathy, and he quickly mixed her a new drink. He set the drink in front of her, took her hand in his, and looked her squarely in the eyes.

"Look. Whatever's wrong I'm not sure this drink is going to help. You want to talk?" She shook her head slowly.

"I'm here if you change your mind," he said as he moved on to other customers.

"Hey, Mary Carol, how are you doing?" asked Susan, a friend of her older sister's, as she took the seat next to her. Mary Carol, her sister, and her brother were all one year apart and always shared friends.

"I'm fine, and what's new with you?" Mary Carol responded flatly.

Wide-eyed, Susan told Mary Carol about an assault that had taken place the night before in Susan's apartment complex.

"Can you believe it?" she asked breathlessly. "Imagine! Robbed and raped not ten steps from your front door. This town sure has changed."

"Don't get so excited," snorted Mary Carol. "You'd probably be happy with the attention." Susan was surprised.

"How can you say that? Being raped is the worst thing that I can imagine. You'd have sexual hangups for years."

Mary Carol straightened her back and pushed her muscular body away from the bar. "No man could ever rape me," she declared. "I'm stronger than most of the wimps around here and, if nothing else, I can outrun them." Susan reminded her that many attackers are armed.

"Then I'd die trying. Only weaklings are taken advantage of, and I'm no pushover. Most women ask to be victims."

Susan was shocked at her insensitive attitude. *She's looking for a fight tonight,* she thought. *What a bore.* "I'll see you later," Susan said as she slid off the stool. "Say hello to your sister for me."

Mary Carol was left brooding over another drink. Instead of cheering her up, people just kept provoking her.

"Hi, honey," Mike said as he grabbed the vacant stool. He had known Mary Carol for many years but never had been able to reach her. He had been willing to give their relationship a chance to grow in high school, but it had gone nowhere. She had been too determined and opinionated. Frankly, he did not know why he was attracted to her at all. He allowed himself a long look at her pretty face and perfect skin, her long neck and lean body.

"Want to dance?" he asked.

"No," was her rude reply. "I'm out of here." She swallowed her drink and her voice softened. "Look. It's not you. It's me. I've got to sort some things out." She gave him a light kiss on the cheek and said goodbye. Less than an hour after she had entered the bar, Mary Carol was outside on the sidewalk looking for a ride.

Gerald Stano just happened to be riding by, pressed his brakes and opened the door. She got in immediately and said, "Just take me west."

He bristled at her terse, taxi-like instructions, but decided to take her west across the river on Seabreeze. He crossed the bridge, went through the big traffic circle, and proceeded west on Mason Avenue. Nothing was said, and he thought her mood was "hell, zero." When she finally requested that they stop at Fanny Farkel's, he ignored her and whizzed on by.

"You'll have to wait. I need cigarettes," he said and headed for Gooding's Grocery. They crossed left into the parking lot, past the Full House Lounge, to Gooding's. Sitting alone in the car, Mary Carol began to feel uncomfortable. When he got back into the car she asked him again to take her to Fanny Farkel's. He did not reply as he began to drive west on Mason Avenue. She became very concerned as the road became lonelier. The match struck for his cigarette briefly lit the black interior, and he exhaled smoke in her face.

"That one's for you," he laughed.

"Damn you," she hissed, and rolled down the window. At that moment he stopped for a traffic light at Clyde Morris Boulevard. "Either turn right and take me home, or take me back," she demanded.

The light seemed endless as he sat very still staring at her, smiling. Suddenly, he put his hand hard on her knee and said, "I want some right here." Her mocking laughter rang out.

"You've got to be kidding," she said sarcastically. She cast a sideways glance and stopped mid chuckle. The look in his eyes frightened her. Now her voice was unsteady. "Who the hell do you think you are, anyway?"

She tried to loosen his grip on her leg, but was startled at his strength. She lunged for the door, but he pulled her back. His left hand found his knife under the seat. Suddenly he went berserk, screaming and stabbing her in the chest. Her body slumped forward but she still had enough strength to again try for the door. Again, he pulled her back, stabbing her repeatedly in the shoulder and lower back. The light changed, and he sped away.

She was making gurgling noises, choking on her own blood, when he passed the hospital, crossed Volusia Avenue, and drove by Mainland High where she had accomplished so much and had so many good times. A last goodbye to life. That was the last thing she saw before dying.

He was thinking only of where he might get rid of her body. Stano intensely disliked the mess she was beginning to make in his car. He remembered the garbage place and turned right on Old Bellevue Road. Finally he came to a dirt road which led to a wooded area. He stopped, left the car running, and pulled her crumpled body out. He got a small piece of carpet from his car and covered her with it. He put leaves and small tree branches over her. Despite the obvious risk of being seen, he lingered over the gruesome tableau he had created. Finally, a screaming jet aircraft taking off from the adjacent Daytona Beach Airport broke his concentration on the body. Pleased with his handiwork, he drove back to Gooding's for more cold beer.

In the light of the shopping center, he realized that Mary Carol's shoes and purse were still in his car. He saw a large dark blue Dumpster by the Full House Lounge and threw in the knife, her shoes, and her handbag. He drove home and diligently went to work scrubbing the bloody mess in his car with bleach and rug cleaner. Soon there was absolutely no trace of his deadly act.

Two Weeks Later

"Hey, where are you going?" Scott asked as Sam suddenly swerved the car onto Old Bellevue Road. They had been heading to the library at the college for a Sunday afternoon study session. Sam obviously had other plans for this clear day in mid February.

"Aw, come on. This is our last chance to kick up some dust before classes begin again tomorrow," Sam complained. He pulled a six-pack of beer out of a paper bag on the backseat, opened one, and drank lustily.

"Have a brewski, loosen up!" Sam laughed. As usual, Scott went along with Sam's change of their plans.

Although similar in age and background, Sam and Scott were a study in contrasts. Sam had dark hair, was lanky and clean shaven. He strutted about, proud of his dark good looks, and his charisma and confidence won him many friends. Scott was heavyset and unremarkable in almost every respect, except for his red hair and freckled complexion which made him seem perpetually sunburned.

Sam pulled off the main road onto a dirt path. He enjoyed riding unrestricted along back roads and was always in search of uncharted territory. They bounced along, drinking beer and recounting adventures which would have required much more time to achieve than their nineteen years.

"Sam, if you hit another hole like that my head will go through the roof! Pull over anyway. I've got to take a leak," Scott said.

"You always did have a pea-sized bladder," laughed Sam.

Scott got out of the car and walked away from the car. Within seconds, Sam heard him crashing though underbrush. Scott ran back to the car, but before he could get in all the way he vomited.

"Damn it, Scott! Not in the car," shouted Sam. Scott was oblivious, gagging and gurgling.

"You never could hold your liquor. What a wimp you are," Sam said in disgust.

"It's not the beer, Sam, it's what I saw over there," gasped his friend.

"What the hell'd you see?"

"I saw a dead body, that's what," whispered Scott. Sam's anger quickly dissipated.

"Maybe he's not dead. We ought to go see if we can help," offered Sam weakly.

"It ain't a he, it's a she and believe me, she's dead. Bones and everything. I picked up what I thought was fur and it turned out to be a ponytail with maggots at the other end. She was covered with branches and stuff. It's the grossest thing I ever saw." Scott was visibly shaken. Whatever it was down there that made Scott puke his guts out must be hideous. Sam shook himself and regained his composure.

"We've got to call the police," he said.

A mile or so away at the police station, Sergeant Paul Crow was getting ready to wind down his shift and go home when the telephone rang. Rarely did it bring good news. *Hell,* he thought, *there goes another evening with the family.* Good thing his wife and son were so understanding.

"We've got a signal 10 on Bellevue out by the airport. It may be one of your missing persons," said the voice on the other end.

"Okay, I'll be there in five minutes." He hung up the phone and rubbed his eyes. His arms were like ham hocks, due to weight lifting. He was solid and strong and good-natured. He had won several lifting competitions and had helped other men train. Crow was of medium height, very compact, and muscular. Then, in his thirties, he was beginning to feel old, especially on days when he had to look at dead bodies. He sighed and collected his belongings.

"Thought you were outta here," joked a fellow officer. Paul Crow smiled but did not respond. His laconic demeanor hid his keen intelligence. Sergeant Crow had served in nearly every division of the police department and had taught police rookie school. Everyone on the force knew him and liked him. Some of the men had known him all his life. He was born in Daytona Beach, and his father ran a fish camp there. At Mainland High, he had been a football star. After school, he enlisted in the Army and fought in Viet Nam. Unlike many others

39

his age, Crow believed in serving his country and his fellow man. After coming home in 1966, he decided the police force would be the best way to contribute. Going to college at night he earned a degree in criminal justice. A hardworking officer, he was rewarded with promotions and opportunities, like the chance to attend the FBI's Homicide Investigation School. His studies in advanced interrogation techniques and criminal psychological profiling made him a better detective.

Crow drove the short distance to the scene. The forensic team had already converged and had begun gathering evidence, measuring and calculating, sketching and photographing. The road was blocked with police vans, patrol cars and barricades. A uniformed officer directed traffic around the barrier and kept the curious at bay. Red lights flashed, and the police radio crackled.

The patrolman waved Crow through the barricade. Yellow tape, stretched from one branch to another, formed a ring around the crime scene.

"How's it going, Art?" Crow asked the coroner.

"It's going okay, Paul. You'll get a full report in the morning," he answered tersely. Everyone on the scene was a professional and had done this countless times. Crow didn't doubt this team's efforts, but he'd have to go see for himself. He was a bulldog on the importance of thoroughness at the crime scene investigation. It was his pet peeve. Many had seen him shake his head and say that the crime scene starts to deteriorate the moment the first uniformed officer arrives there. Some didn't like that kind of talk, but Crow didn't give a damn. He'd throw any punch that got the job done. It was his style to work outside the conventional circle; to think like the predator; to move like him, slowly, thoroughly; overlooking nothing, analyzing everything.

He slowly walked the fifty yards down the dirt road until he reached a small canal. Turning east on another path that ran along the canal, he went another fifty yards through palmetto brush to the body. The woods were completely thick with pine trees and palmetto scrub so that the body was completely hidden from Bellevue Road and the dirt roads.

The smell got unbearable as Crow drew closer. He put his handkerchief over his nose and mouth. The body had been there at least two weeks, judging from the state of decomposition. What struck Crow was the deliberate staging of the scene. The body was laid out with the head pointing in a northerly direction. A piece of carpet partially covered the corpse. Small trees and branches had been cut and carefully arranged over the body.

The gold Seiko watch on the bony arm had stopped on January 30. He also noted that the clothing was in good shape but that the shoes were missing. On her breast bone and left side of the chest were several small holes and one large one. These appeared to have been made by a sharp pointed object. There was another hole in the center of her back, about bra level, and another mark in her lower middle back. Although some of her flesh was gone, the clothes were intact and blood covered what were apparently stab wounds. *The murder had been an act of rage,* Crow deduced. The killer had spent a lot of effort decorating and arranging the body, but had not really tried to hide it.

How could she have stab wounds there? he pondered as he made little jabs in the air. *Doesn't make any sense at all. Maybe he came around this way.* For a long time he considered the angles of the wounds. The thing that jumped out at him was the similarity of other cases he remembered throughout the years of girls found in Tomoka State Park. He had seen enough. Crow knew he had a crazy on the loose.

When Crow returned to the police department, he checked the records division for missing persons reports. Using the physical and clothing descriptions as reference and comparing them to what had been discovered at the body's site, including the watch, he determined that the body could be Mary Carol Maher's.

Crow produced a psychological profile of her killer: male, white, and not much over thirty; lives in the Daytona Beach area and knows it well; works at a common job and drives an ordinary car; is meticulously clean, probably compulsively so; is ritualistic; picks up hitchhikers and hookers; has a hot temper, hates women, and cannot take rejection; does not always rape or rob, but may keep shoes or purses as trophies; is strong and smart enough to outmaneuver and butcher a well-conditioned female athlete; and has killed before and will kill again. A lot was known about the man, but the question remained: Who in the hell was he?

Three

February-April 1980

Valentine's Day had been anything but a sweetheart of a time for twenty-six year old Toni Van Haddocks. She had lived for six years with a black man who forced her to continue working as a hooker. She was tired of the rat race and wanted someone to take care of her for a change. A few months ago, she thought that he might let her quit when he learned that she was pregnant. But he was furious with her for getting pregnant and slapped her around. She fell on her arm and broke it, and it was in a cast now.

Last night he beat her again. He was meaner than a pit bull when he drank, and today her arm hurt like hell. Her life seemed irreversibly screwed up. Her three small children were left with her mother to raise. God only knew what her mother would say about this new baby if it ever lived to full term. Her mother had a job with the city and tried hard to lead a decent life. Toni knew that she had been a great disappointment, but although she was

44

ashamed, she was powerless to change.

Toni usually walked the streets around North and Ridgewood near the 7-Eleven store. Business was fairly good at this location, near the strip joints and topless bars.

She knew she looked attractive in her tan slacks and brown blouse. Her brown leather jacket was tossed over her shoulder. Toni flicked her long black hair a few times with her good arm and started walking slowly toward the Shingle Shack at Madison Avenue. It was nine o'clock and quiet.

Toni's usual method of operation was to get twenty dollars up front and have her customer drive to a close, secluded spot near the railroad track at Hazel Street. There were some abandoned houses there and nobody ever bothered her. She felt safe there because she had visited the place so often.

Ridgewood was also the street where Stano lived. This Friday night, as he usually did after work, he had drunk a few beers. Now, he was cruising down Ridgewood with his car windows down and stereo blaring. He noticed Toni, and, by the way she moved, he thought correctly that she was offering something for sale.

Jerry turned down the stereo and offered her thirty dollars. His generous offer allowed him to pay later. Actually, he had no money and did not intend to pay.

Toni agreed and was ready to go. In complete control of the situation and enjoying his game, he headed for a partially developed area near a house that his father owned. Jerry used to live in the house; now his brother lived there. He was constantly looking for ways to hurt his brother, who was eighteen months younger and also adopted.

"Hey, man, where are you taking me?" Toni said as he turned down a dirt road. It was very dark, and Toni was getting scared. Usually she just went a few blocks, performed, and got back to her working street to look for another customer.

Silently, he smiled, chain-smoked and kept time with the music. Halfway down the dirt road, he turned onto a smaller side road and went about fifty yards. Toni complained again nervously. Her left arm was uncomfortable in the cast. He had bumped it several times and apologized, but now he laughed and hit her arm again. She cried out in pain, and tears ran down her cheeks. He stopped the car abruptly, forced her face into his lap and demanded a blow job.

When she had finished, she meekly asked for her money. He angered at her bluntness. His left hand grasped the knife by his seat. With an inhuman scream, he plunged the knife deep into her. Her large, brown eyes widened in shock and pain. He pulled the knife out of her with his right hand and stabbed her again. He did not want to mess up his upholstery so he pulled her twitching body out of the car and stood over her as she moaned. Screaming in a killing frenzy, he stabbed her thirty-eight times in the head. She stopped making any sound. Having spent himself, he took a few moments to catch his breath. Then, he dragged the body away from the car and covered it with palm fronds and tree branches. Faintly he heard a dog howling, and momentarily stopped to listen.

Stano started the car, backed out of the narrow dirt road, and drove to his brother's house nearby. He was tired and considered staying there for the night, but the lights were out and he went back to his own room. He removed his blood spattered T-shirt, and sponged off the blood on the seat of his car. Then he wrapped the knife in the shirt, locked it all in the car trunk, and went to bed. The game was over and Toni Van Haddocks was forgotten.

When Toni did not return home to her boyfriend all weekend, he reported her missing. He told police he had left her on the street Friday night and that she never returned home. On Wednesday, the police contacted a reporter for the local newspaper and provided a picture and missing person story. Toni's boyfriend cooperated with the police, and accompanied two detectives to the area of Charles and Hazel Streets around the railroad tracks to look for clues. None were found.

During the next several weeks, some leads and false sightings were followed up with no results. Someone reported having seen a pregnant black female with her arm in a cast with a white man in a brown car. This and similar reports were all dead ends. Meanwhile, for the Daytona police their search continued.

Four

March 1980

It was four o'clock in the morning on March 25, 1980, as a sullen Gerald Stano rode down Ocean Avenue looking for action. He disliked women in general, and hated prostitutes in particular. Stano got more pleasure beating women up than having sex with them. The word was out around the Loop that he was mean and most prostitutes stayed clear. Donna Hensley had been with him but she was usually so high on drugs that she didn't remember.

Tonight Donna was stoned again, standing beneath the lights of the Blue Grass Hotel. Her long, straight hair covered scars on her earlobes where pierced earrings had been ripped. Her face was blank; her eyes vacant. At twenty-six, she had been a prostitute for six years, and it showed. Jerry saw her, stopped, and they struck a deal. She got in the car and they rode the one block back to her motel room.

The Tower Motel was old, and conversations could be heard through the thin walls. Tonight it was relatively quiet as they entered the room. Stano removed his flashy pants and folded them neatly. They sat on the bed and smoked a joint. Slowly she unbuttoned his neatly pressed shirt and laid it on the chair beside his trousers. She tried to arouse him, rubbing his small penis but Jerry didn't react normally. He could not perform sexually, and he knew it. When he heard her mocking laughter, his anger exploded.

He leaped out of bed and started clawing at the clothing in her closet. Throwing the clothes to the floor, he slapped her down on the pile. Donna was terrified. Stano jerked the dresser drawers out and scattered the contents. A four-inch knife dropped to the floor. Instantly they scrambled for the knife, but he reached it first. He stabbed her in the chest. She made only muffled cries for fear that he would cut her deeper. He found a can opener and nail file and pounded them into her arms and thighs; with scissors he slashed her breasts. Donna cried out, and the room started to spin. When he ran to the kitchen, she crawled closer to the hall door. Under the sink, Stano found a bottle of muriatic acid and stumbled back with it. She had made it to the hall, bleeding and screaming for help. Suddenly, Stano grabbed his clothes and his money from her bureau and ran out the back door.

Police arrived and followed the ambulance to Halifax Hospital where Donna was treated for about thirty stab wounds. After her wounds were treated, the police asked Hensley to look at photographs of suspects. She studied dozens of mug shots and at last identified Stano as her assailant. Although other girls had been hurt and terrified by this man, tonight Donna Hensley had the nerve to do what no one else had. She filed charges against her attacker saying, "I may be a whore, but nobody does this to me and gets away with it."

The police quickly learned that Gerald Stano frequently picked up prostitutes and female hitch-hikers, particularly from the Loop on the beach-side. They talked to several local prostitutes including Crystal. Stano had been a customer of hers several weeks before Donna's attack. After they had finished having sex and she was paid, Crystal said that Stano became irate and de-manded his money back. When she argued, he be-came more angry and kicked her out of the car. Then he pulled a gun and shot at her as she fled. Another hooker, Kim, reported that Jerry tried to strangle her and that he had a reputation for vio-lence among hookers.

Based upon Donna's identification, police ob-tained a warrant for the arrest of Gerald Stano on aggravated assault charges. He was arrested at Hampton's Restaurant on Mason Avenue at about ten o'clock on April 1, 1980. His employers and coworkers were amazed when the police hand-cuffed Jerry, read him his rights, and took him away. He had been flipping burgers one minute and in police custody the next.

Detective Paul Crow realized striking similarities in the Hensley assault and the Maher murder. The wounds inflicted were similar, and both girls disappeared from the same beachfront block. For these reasons, Crow sat in the corner of the interview room and watched quietly but intently as another officer questioned Stano. After little more than an hour, Stano confessed to the attack on Donna. By this time, Crow could read Jerry's gestures like a book. When telling the truth, Stano would pull his chair close and lean on the metal table. When about to lie, he would push his chair back, fold his arms and cross his legs. Years as a police officer and specialized training made Paul Crow an expert in reading human behavior.

Crow, who continually stressed the importance of the interview, stated that he "liked to walk a thin line within the constitutional boundaries." The rules are unclear and ever-shifting, so most officers stayed far from any borderline behavior. Not Crow. He knew just where the line was and flirted with the edge. He knew he upset a lot of people with his methods, but it didn't matter. He got results.

"I don't stay within the dots of the known circle of procedure. The killer doesn't stay within those dots. In this case I wasn't dealing with a mom or dad killing each other over the weekend, not dealing with a lover's quarrel or grocery store armed robbery. I was dealing with a felon who was saying: 'I'm going to outthink you. I'm going to outplay you. I'm going to outdo you in every respect.' To me he throws down the gauntlet when he does that. I love that challenge! Some say you can't lie to this guy. I say, who says you can't? You have to be creative."

As he looked into the dark depths of Stano's eyes, Crow decided it was time for him to move in. He tossed down a picture of Mary Carol and her sister.

"Ever seen her?" Crow asked almost nonchalantly. Jerry smiled and leaned on the table. He looked at Crow sidelong through his cigarette smoke.

"Yeah, I knew her," Jerry finally responded, pointing to Mary Carol. The past tense was not lost on Crow. Their eyes locked. Crow knew he was looking at a murderer. Jerry thought he had finally found a friend.

"I thought so," Crow said, smiling. He intimated that the police already had evidence that Stano killed Mary Carol. To win his confidence, Crow led Jerry to think that the police appreciated being rid of the hookers and druggies that had been mysteriously disappearing from the beachside. Crow played upon Stano's long suppressed, burning desire to brag about his conquests. For years, Jerry had no one to tell about his encounters. Now he had an eager ear. For someone confessing to murder, he was strangely happy. Paul Crow was going to become his best friend. With no prompting, Stano described Mary Carol and her last minutes on earth.

Stano stood up to give Mary Carol's height and

weight by gesture and described her as being tall and athletic. When Crow said that Maher was wearing slacks and a shirt, Stano corrected him and said she was wearing jeans and a black shirt with animal designs. This was significant since the missing person report and newspaper accounts had erroneously listed a tan blouse and black slacks. Crow knew Stano had been with Mary Carol.

Jerry described how he had stabbed Mary Carol in the chest as hard as he could, and had stabbed her in the thigh and the back. Again, Crow knew the autopsy report showed a broken sternum and the wounds Stano detailed, except for the back wounds. Finally he told about where he drove and how he left the body near the airport, wrapped in foam padding or ticking and had put branches over it.

Within three hours of his arrest for the aggravated assault of Donna Hensley, Stano signed a formal confession to Mary Carol Maher's murder. Crow got in a police vehicle with Stano in the front seat and Detective Jim Gadberry in the back. Jerry gave directions. After Stano led Crow to a dump site south of the airport, they reached a place where three roads presented a choice. Stano picked the least traveled road to follow. The brush was thick and they proceeded on foot. Stano directed them to the exact location where the body had been found.

When they returned to the Daytona Beach Police

Department, Gadberry bragged that he had solved the Maher case. Several officers who followed in a second car reported to Captain Powers that Stano led them right to the location where the body was found and then cried.

After Stano's confession Crow had a second autopsy of Mary Carol Maher performed. He and the medical examiner went to the funeral home where the coroner examined the body and found for the first time the two stab wounds in her back. These two back wounds, which Stano described in his confession, were missed in the first autopsy report. Stano's detailed knowledge was proven.

Stano was formally booked for aggravated assault and murder in the first degree. While he was in a holding cell, a policeman entered to book a shoplifting suspect. Stano persistently tried to get the officer's attention. When the officer came near him, Stano asked for a match. He smiled and proudly added, "You know, I'm charged with murder."

The officer did a double take.

"Sure you are," he said, pausing long enough to light his cigarette.

"Damn straight," the jailer said from the desk. "He *is* booked on murder."

The policeman returned to talk to Jerry, who was reveling in his newfound notoriety.

"I killed that girl you found on Bellevue Road," he said eagerly.

"Why in God's name did you do that?" the officer asked incredulously.

"I can't stand bitchy chicks. I don't take shit from no broad," Stano announced, "and I cut her." He made stabbing motions to punctuate the point. He had finally found an audience that was attentive to his stories. The thrill of the tale was almost as intoxicating as the killing itself. He was going to enjoy this part, too.

Five

April 1980

Gerald Stano's mother was shocked into numb disbelief by the telephone call from the Daytona Beach police telling her that her son had confessed to murder. Acknowledging the information and hanging up the phone, she thought for a long time in silence. How would she tell her husband? What could they do?

How happy they had been to adopt Jerry that April day in 1952. Instead of a celebration, Norma felt as if someone had died. She was thirty-four then, her husband thirty-eight; they had lost hope of finding a baby.

The baby had been the fifth child of six born to his natural mother, on September 12, 1951, in Schenectady, New York. The healthy boy, almost nine pounds, was named Paul. His mother was an alcoholic and incapable of caring for him. She was promiscuous and spent her days and nights drinking and carousing. His father was never around. When Paul was six-and-a-half months old, his

56

mother asked the Schenectady County Department of Social Services to offer him for adoption. Jerry was not her husband's child and had begun to look different from his siblings. She had already placed three other children with the agency, a fourth child was brain damaged, and one daughter was living at home.

Norma Stano remembered the first time she saw her baby. It was painful to recall. He was malnourished, and had been horribly neglected physically and emotionally. Caseworkers' records showed him to be functioning at an animalistic level. His diaper had not been changed for weeks, and he played with his own feces. This habit would continue until he was a toddler.

Norma had been a social worker and a nurse. Her husband, Eugene, had a good job as a district sales manager for a large corporation. Everything looked positive during the six-month-trial period that they had the baby. But when they went back to the agency to finalize the adoption, they learned that a team had examined the boy.

This team, composed of a psychiatric social worker, nurse, physician, psychologist, and psychiatrist, had determined that the thirteen-month-old boy was unadoptable due to the severe neglect he'd suffered. In desperation, the Stanos enlisted the help of a caseworker and the staff psychologist. Eventually they were allowed to adopt Jerry.

But as he grew, he developed problems. As a

small boy, Jerry never showed affection toward anyone. He had only been interested in things, never in people or their feelings. He wet the bed every night until he was nine years old. Doctors could never give any medical reason for his behavior. Jerry was clumsy and slow to talk, but he was observant. A compulsively neat older child who wanted everything in order, he would pitch a temper tantrum if even one piece of furniture was out of its usual place.

When Jerry was eighteen months old, the Stanos adopted a son named Roger. They tried to make a comfortable home for the boys in their two-story red brick cottage. The tree lined street was a perfect setting for living happily ever after. The neighborhood was friendly and Zoller Elementary was just across the street. Jerry entered kindergarten there on September 10, 1956. His antisocial behavior began there; he didn't want to share the teacher's attention so he bit and punched the other students. His parents decided to send him to first grade at Brown, a private school. He passed the first grade there, but had to repeat second grade. Jerry returned to public school in 1960, but things did not go smoothly.

He was actively disliked by his classmates, had no friends, and could not relate to anyone. Even in the sixth grade, he was polite, but unable to control himself without supervision. In late 1964, the Stanos moved to Mount Vernon, New York, and Jerry enrolled in Traphagen Junior High School. By this time he had turned in false fire alarms, and had dropped a large rock from a highway overpass onto a car to smash its windshield. Westchester County juvenile authorities warned his parents that a third offense would mean the reformatory for Gerald.

Desperately looking for a solution, the Stanos sent Jerry to Hargrove Military Academy in Chatham, Virginia. Trouble began there almost immediately. He borrowed large sums of money from various cadets and refused to repay them. He quickly alienated the cadets, who bullied him and teased him about his weight, his thick glasses, and the fact that he was so easily frightened. He was a C and D student; his only good subject was music.

Disappointed, his parents pulled Jerry out of Hargrove and sent him to his grandparents in Ormond Beach, Florida. There he attended Seabreeze Junior High for two years. Norma remembered that when she picked him up from her parents' house, they had installed locks on their bedroom door. A disturbing fact on which they refused to elaborate.

In 1967 the family moved to Pennsylvania. Their home was between the blue-collar city of Norristown and the rolling hills of suburban Ambler. But even in this comfortable setting, they again had difficulty with Jerry. He had stolen money from his father's wallet, and had paid members of the track team to run behind him so that he would not finish last. He continuously skipped school and had difficulties with his classmates when he did attend. Truancy, lying, and petty theft continued throughout his years at Shady Grove Junior High and Wissahickon High School. Perhaps his only positive experiences were playing bass clarinet in the marching band and singing in the choir. Finally at age twenty-one, he received his high school diploma.

Soon after Jerry's return from Florida, the Stanos began having problems with Jerry's adopted brother, Roger, who was popular and made good grades in school. Roger ran away from home twice. Roger told his parents that he would "crack up" if he had to stay around Jerry, whom he thought was devious and mean.

At the family's insistence, Jerry moved to a motel. He decided to go to computer school at Maxwell Institute, and after finishing that, he went to work in the computer room at Chestnut Hill Hospital. He lost the job because he stole money from employees' purses. Next, he went to work in the computer department of the University of Pennsylvania, where he lied about his experience and training in order to get the job. When faced with the truth, he continued to lie and was consequently fired.

Shortly after being fired from the university, he was thrown out of his hotel for stealing money from other rooms. At this point, he returned to his family's home to live. He went to work for Burroughs Corporation, but soon was fired for being totally incorrigible. Jerry had gotten a retarded girl pregnant and had to pay for an abortion. Her father threatened Jerry with a gun. Jerry started drinking heavily, experimenting with drugs, and running around. His behavior, when drinking, ranged from a happy, silly drunk to a deranged madman.

After the Burroughs fiasco, his father again took Jerry to Florida where his mother was caring for her ailing mother. Jerry immediately began to get into trouble drinking, forging checks, and stealing. The Stanos paid for him to take a hotel management course at Daytona Beach Community College. He dropped out. He was described as making a great first impression and then sliding downhill. He was an enthusiastic starter, but never finished anything.

Over the next seven years, he took a variety of jobs. He pumped gas at several stations, was a hotel clerk, worked in a Montgomery Ward and at Howard Johnson's. He delivered soda for Canada Dry, was a short-order cook, and bound publications for the local newspaper. He had average looks, not sinister or repulsive, but he was unpopular with girls.

During 1975 he met and dated a twenty-two-year-old local hairstylist. They were married on June 21, 1975 at the Prince of Peace Catholic Church in Ormond Beach. Jerry was on probation for stealing and needed permission to leave Volusia County for his honeymoon. The Stanos were hopeful that the marriage would result in a happy solution to their problems with Gerald.

One week after their honeymoon, the couple returned to their two-bedroom mobile home on Timbercreek Road, north of Daytona Beach. Jerry went to work for his father-in-law at the Shell Station on U.S. 1. They started having problems immediately. He physically abused his wife, and, on at least one occasion, choked her. In a fit of anger he attempted to strangle her poodle and shot and killed her horse. In March, 1976, Gerald and his wife tried psychological counseling with Robert Davis, a local doctor.

By this time, however, the marriage was over. His wife left him in August, filed for divorce in September, and it was granted to her in November. She got one car; he got the other. They sold their double-wide mobile home. Jerry returned to his parents' home to live.

After the divorce, Jerry continued to drink and have violent periods. He continued to use his parents as he had done so successfully all his life. During the following year, he lived in two different homes owned by his father in Holly Hill, just north of Daytona. In the next two years, 1978 and 1979, he lived in several small apartments on Ridgewood Avenue in Daytona and Ormond Beach.

All of this seemed like a bad dream to Norma Stano today. She had overlooked so much concerning Jerry in the past. Now she had to face the awful prospect that perhaps he was capable of murder. Regardless of how desperately she wanted to believe otherwise, she had to admit that Jerry was a problem of increasing seriousness as the years passed. With bitter tears, she realized that she had lived in dreadful expectation. Now, God forgive her, she was almost relieved.

Norma and Eugene Stano braced themselves after the initial news that their son had been arrested. They went to the jail to try to help him. Mrs. Stano took the position that the boy she raised was not a murderer. The Stanos decided to hire Donald Jacobson, their family lawyer, to defend their son.

Six

April-May 1980

"Norma Stano is on line two," said Maggie, poking her head through the partially open door. Don Jacobson automatically smiled at his secretary although he guessed this was no laughing matter. He sighed, punched the phone line, and eased back into his leather chair. Through sobs, Norma told him that Jerry was in big trouble now. He'd been arrested for the murder of a local girl. She was frantic for more information. He tried to calm her down and assured her that he would find out what details he could and call back. With a low whistle, Jacobson realized that Jerry's long anticipated dark side had finally come to light.

He was not really surprised by the phone call from the Stanos. For years he had represented Jerry on a variety of charges including traffic tickets, bad checks, and soliciting prostitutes. Now he was accused of murder.

* * *

Jacobson was a colorful character. His well tailored suits and extravagant life-style reflected his significant income. He was a small man who moved gracefully. His manner seemed studied from a film personality of his era such as Douglas Fairbanks, Jr. The mustachioed smile and quick wit made him popular with the ladies. In fact, he had been married several times. His charm was always present even in stressful times. He had handled many capital cases since opening his law office in Daytona Beach, and had become well-known as a flamboyant criminal defense attorney. His successes enabled him to pursue the hobby of owning and racing expensive sports cars, which included a special edition Porsche.

After his training as a naval fighter pilot, he graduated from Stetson Law School. For the next several years he served with the FBI under J. Edgar Hoover as a special liaison agent to the Truman White House. In 1959, he began his private law practice in Daytona Beach.

Jacobson, who believed strongly in genetics, thought that murderers were born preprogrammed to kill. He had seen nothing in Jerry's behavioral history to indicate otherwise. The case would definitely be a challenge. Perhaps he could keep Stano alive using a defense of insanity.

As promised, Don went to visit Jerry in jail. He greeted the guards with his automatic smile. As a criminal defense attorney, Jacobson was a frequent visitor to the jail. He signed in.

"Here to see that wacko?" asked the guard when he read the log. Jacobson smiled. "You'll have to narrow it down more than that," he replied. The deputy grunted in agreement and pushed the button to open the heavy gate.

The jail door creaked and moaned as it rolled open. Jacobson walked down the dismal corridor he'd traveled many times. He waved at friendly faces behind the bars. Finally he came to the interview room where attorneys can have some privacy with their clients. Jerry was waiting.

Jacobson looked through the window in the door for a moment before turning the doorknob. The room was small and sparsely decorated with two ancient wooden chairs and a small table. Jerry was pacing like a caged animal, biting his fingernails and furiously smoking a cigarette. Jacobson hoped that he could weather the long storm ahead, but he doubted Jerry had the strength.

Jerry almost jumped on Jacobson when he entered the room. A familiar face was a welcome sight. "Don, you've got to get me out of here! I'm going crazy! Please help me untangle this mess! They arrested me at work and now my boss will surely fire me and—"

Don held up his hand and stopped Stano mid sentence. "Slow down, Jerry. Wait a minute. Just relax and start at the beginning. We've got plenty of time now." Jacobson spoke in soothing tones.

"Get me out of here NOW," ordered Jerry, his eyes growing cold. "There's no bond set yet. You're my lawyer. Do something or else . . ." his voice trailed off, his thought left hanging.

"You're charged with a capital offense, not shoplifting. There is no bond set most of the time." Jacobson realized that Jerry had no idea of the seriousness of the situation. This case was not like the others they had together. "Before a bond can be set, we have to show that the evidence is weak and that its unlikely that the state can convict you. That's more difficult after a confession." Jacobson smiled wryly.

"She was a whore. I gave her just what she deserved." Jerry spat out the words while making stabbing motions with his cigarette. "Damn right I killed her." Jacobson finally knew what he had long feared and suspected: He was looking at an hysterical man who had committed murder. They spoke a few more minutes, and Jacobson rose to leave.

"Tell Mom and Dad that I love them," choked Jerry through tears. Jacobson sighed and promised to return the next day.

Jacobson told the Stanos later that there was a hidden side of their son, another Jerry, and that his best chance of receiving treatment and beating the charges was to bring out that hidden side. The Stanos hoped that they could also help Jerry by getting him psychiatric treatment. They remembered that Jacobson and a local criminal psychologist, Ann McMillan, successfully defended David Hester in the witchcraft cult murders in Volusia County in the 1970s by having him declared insane.

Jacobson believed that they had to have more knowledge of him and more confessions in order to either obtain a deal from the court or to succeed with an insanity defense. They talked about personality profiles and Jerry's lack of remorse or pity for his victims. The Stanos finally agreed to have Dr. McMillan begin an extensive study of their son.

Don knew that Jerry had a complex mind. Sometimes he would talk to you openly; sometimes he would not. He could be very amiable and polite enough to stand when others entered the room. Yet, at the slightest provocation, he could change into a mean, cruel person. Jacobson suspected that many times when the family had moved during Jerry's younger years it was because of some sort of violent behavior by Jerry. He would soon learn much about his client that he would not reveal for many years.

Years later Jacobson said that it had been difficult to bear the knowledge of so many confessions, some in other states, beginning when Jerry was only seventeen years old. "This is the way it is with most serial killers like Jerry Stano, and I've known many," Jacobson said later. "They are very complicated, but they are genetic. Once you can buy that, then you can appreciate what the lay public is going to be so distressed to hear: that you can take this youngster, just a boy, and if you know enough about him you can put a tag on his forehead, Serial Killer."

On April 3, the police impounded Jerry's car and sent it to the Sanford Crime Lab where it was dismantled in a search for evidence. Paul Crow was convinced that Stano was guilty not only of the Maher murder, but of others. The police searched his room at the Riviera Motel, but found nothing. His mother was encouraged. She always washed Jerry's clothes and believed she would have seen bloodstains if there had been any. His motel room was clean and neat, just like his car and person. This was a puzzlement. Had someone else been there before the investigators to rearrange the room? There were no knives, no guns, no victim's property or anything else to corroborate or support his confessions. The detectives interrogated Stano over the next several days but their efforts were fruitless. He was now mute.

Jerry's attitude in jail was predictable. He now maintained his innocence. He told his lawyer that his confessions were forced. He asked advice on what to tell Crow when he questioned him again. In letters to his parents, he asked for their forgiveness, love, and permission to return home. He asked his brother to take care of their mom and dad. In letters to friends, he fondly recalled the Riviera Motel Coffee Shop and told them of his new life in jail.

On April 14, 1980, Gerald Eugene Stano was indicted for the first-degree murder of Mary Carol Maher. There was still no evidence except his confession. This situation changed, however, when his involvement in the Toni Van Haddocks murder became known.

On Tuesday, April 15, a twelve-year-old boy found a human skull in the woods behind his house. Terrified, he ran home and took his older brother back to the place of the discovery. They carried the skull home on the end of a stick and called the sheriff's department. When the police arrived, they went to the scene at about seven in the evening. The excited boys showed them exactly where in the undeveloped part of the subdivision they had found the skull. There, scattered about, were other human bones. While there was still enough light, photographs were taken, the area was roped off, and a deputy was posted to guard the crime scene overnight.

The next day, two technicians from the crime lab in Sanford were summoned. With the help of investigators, the four systematically walked and mapped the five acres of open ground where bones were found. They were soon joined by Florida Department of Law Enforcement representatives and reporters from local television stations.

As bones were found, flags went down to mark the spots. It became obvious that animals had moved bones and had chewed and scratched them. The heavy undergrowth made the search more difficult.

On Saturday, several vacant lots away from where the first bones were found, a neighborhood boy located the victim's spinal column. The next day he found the lower torso of a human, a blouse, a bra, and a forearm in a cast. Branches covered the area where these items were found. Body fluids had stained the earth, killing the foliage beneath it. The new findings were photographed, marked with tape, and that area was sealed.

On Sunday night Detective Paul Crow came to the scene. He and the other detectives tentatively identified the cast, clothing, and remains collected during the week as those of Toni Van Haddocks. Later, the medical examiner confirmed with an X ray that the teeth were Toni's. After a final search for evidence, the scene was secured — a full week after the initial discovery and over nine weeks after the young woman's disappearance.

The discovery of Toni Van Haddocks's remains did not go unnoticed by Stano. The fantastic story received broad coverage in the local news. He was beginning to feel trapped.

To rule out natural causes of death and to determine which marks were made by animals, Toni's remains were sent to the Anthropology Lab at Florida State University. The resulting report cataloged animal damage to the bones and noted four significant facts. First, there were thirty-eight knife cuts or punctures to the skull, which occurred at or near the time of death. Second, these puncture wounds were not due to animals and could not have been self-inflicted. Third, homicide appeared to be the most likely cause of death because of the concealment of the remains and nature of the wounds to the skull. Finally, there was a near full-term fetus in the pelvis.

Stano's parents continued to visit him over the next several weeks. He was told that Dr. McMillan would see him on May 8 at the recommendation of his lawyer. Jerry wrote to his parents on Mother's Day from the jail. He thanked them for their visits and bringing books. "Without loving parents, it would be difficult to face what is in store for me," he wrote.

As promised, on May 8, Dr. Ann McMillan interviewed the Stanos for three and one half hours, reviewed substantiating documents, and spent over six hours interviewing and evaluating Jerry. She concluded that he had never had a normal personality. He had no emotions, feelings, or conscience, and never had normal male-female relationships. All of his girlfriends had some abnormality. Two were retarded; one was an epileptic; others were runaways or prostitutes. Jerry's abnormal behavior and antisocial acts followed a consistent progression from infancy to adulthood that made the act of murder a logical rather than illogical event. Dr. McMillan believed that Jerry was schizophrenic. Unnecessary ferocity and senselessness are the hallmarks of a schizophrenic murderer. He will probably kill more than one person and acts out of intolerable anger and frustration, as demonstrated by the violence of his murders. The schizophrenic's calm lack of remorse and emotional detachment after his bizarre murders are explained by the degree of his alienation from society. The violence involved in his acts produces a sense of gratification and peace.

Seven

June 1980-March 1981

The meeting with McMillan made Jerry hopeful of receiving psychiatric treatment. His parents wanted to believe that he could be cured. They wanted to believe that treatment could absolve his acts. Jerry wanted to avoid the electric chair, be hospitalized, then get released.

The next day a meeting was held in Jacobson's law office, attended by the Stanos, Crow, Jacobson, his investigator, and McMillan. A discussion ensued regarding several open homicide cases, including Van Haddocks. They all decided to try to get Jerry to confess to all crimes he had committed in an effort to arrange a plea bargain.

The scheme developed by Jacobson was working. The defense team would assist the police in getting confessions from Stano and, in return, Jerry would receive hospitalization or life imprisonment. Jacobson formally petitioned the court for the appointment of mental health experts to determine Stano's competency to stand trial. Doctors

McMillan, Stern, and Davis were appointed by the court.

Crow went to interview Stano in the county jail. Stano was re-advised of his constitutional rights, signed a waiver form, and agreed to discuss the Haddocks case. He freely admitted committing the Van murder and told the story of the pickup, stabbing, and ritualistic burial. He had now confessed to two murders with no other evidence against him.

The police were frustrated by their lack of supporting evidence. They were also stymied in their efforts to obtain more information from Jerry. Although they had the help of his parents, attorney, and psychologist, no new information was obtained for several weeks. When he asked, the detectives told Jerry that they had withheld disclosing his confession in the Toni Van Haddocks case in order to protect him from being harmed by black prisoners in the jail. They pretended to protect him from New Jersey and Pennsylvania authorities who wanted to question him about unsolved murders in their states. They told him that he needed protection from other inmates and promised extra privileges if he would cooperate in solving unsolved crimes. He believed more confessions would add credence to his insanity defense. Stano was flattered by Crow's constant attention. The strategy of the defense team was to stall for time, isolate Stano, and have only Crow talk to him. In this manner, Crow should be able to get more confessions. His parents agreed to the plan.

Over the next several months, Stano wrote to his lawyer often. He proposed several preposterous plans, including life probation and banishment from the State of Florida. Once he realized that there was actually no evidence other than his confessions, he tried to overcome them with lie detector tests, alibis, and character witnesses. Stano's attitude gradually changed. His complaints about jail space, medical treatment, and possible harm to himself reflected his growing dislike of confinement. His mental outlook about possible outcomes of his situation evolved. At first, he claimed that his confessions were coerced and could be easily suppressed. Then he realized that they were being taken seriously, and his hope changed from release to a successful insanity defense to avoid life imprisonment or the electric chair. He was beginning to adopt the viewpoint of the defense team. His best option was to make a deal.

Stano was examined for competency by Doctors Stern and Davis in early June. The law requires doctors to make specific findings concerning a criminal defendant's mental competency to stand trial. Both doctors agreed that Stano was competent, that he understood the nature of the charges and the nature of the penalties. However, he had no concern about the seriousness of the offenses, no major denial and no remorse. He blamed his anger and his violent behavior on the belligerence of his victims. Stano was motivated to help himself and capable of assisting his attorney in the preparation of his defense, according to the psychiatrists. He did not qualify under the statutory criteria for involuntary confinement to a mental hospital. The doctors concluded that he was a candidate for a diagnosis of schizophrenic disorder after additional evaluation.

On March 2, 1981, a meeting was held between Crow, McMillan, Jacobson, and Stano's father. All were convinced that Stano knew much more than he had told. After the meeting, Mr. Stano visited his son in the DeLand Jail and tearfully begged him to confess to all his murders. Jerry told his father of four more women he had murdered in the local area. The next day, Jerry wrote to Jacobson, told him of his talk with his father, and provided more details of the murders. Jacobson relayed the new information to Detective Crow, but they were outside of Crow's jurisdiction of the Daytona Beach city limits. However, when the details were relayed to Dave Hudson of the Volusia County Sheriff's Office, the confessions matched four unsolved murder cases.

On March 12, Stano met with Sgt. Crow and Detective Dave Hudson. Hudson had files on four unsolved Volusia County cases. Although he did not know the victims' names, Stano could supply matching data on clothing, employment, friends, homes, and, most importantly, burial sites. Crow was attentive as the two men exchanged information about four additional murders. Stano gave taped confessions to the murders.

The next day, on March 13, 1981, Hudson, Crow, and Stano drove to Tomoka State Park, an area composed of miles of natural vegetation. Stano directed the route through a maze of back roads to the location where he left the body. Hudson confirmed that this was the location where Ramona Neal, 18, was found. Next, Stano directed the officers to drive to a set of power lines two miles away. Stano referred to this area as Cobb's Corner. Hudson confirmed that this was where the body of twenty-four-year-old Nancy Heard was found. Later that day, Stano gave specific descriptions of how he had left two of his other victims, sixteen-year-old Linda Ann Hamilton on the beach at Turtle Mound and Jane Doe, an unidentified prostitute, along the Highway I-95 median.

Stano had now confessed to six murders:

> Mary Carol Maher, 1980
> Toni Van Haddocks, 1980
> Ramona Neal, 1976
> Jane Doe, 1978
> Nancy Heard, 1975
> Linda Ann Hamilton, 1975

Slowly, Crow earned Jerry's confidence. Although Stano tried to prolong the enjoyment of being the center of attention, Crow was obtaining valuable information. He had no idea how much of the iceberg was visible: just how much was Stano holding back? Crow's curiosity got the best of him during the March 13, 1981 interview.

"Since 1973 until 1980, just how many women could you estimate that you killed?" he asked directly.

Jerry smiled and leaned forward as he took a drag on his cigarette. Even Crow was surprised when he responded, "Between two and four per. . . . Change that. Make it between four and six per year."

Eight

January 1975

She had been knocking around since she was a teenager. With her long blond hair, large green eyes and trim figure, she looked like a child of the 60s and 70s. She liked to drink wine, smoke pot and listen to folk guitars. Along the way she had left a marriage on the rocks at Myrtle Beach, and was presently working as a maid at the Mandarin Motel on the beach at Daytona. She was searching for answers, and she found comfort in the nearness of the ocean. Somehow she identified with the sea gulls and pelicans swirling over the water, hustling for survival. This job was a dead end and paid very little. However, it did give her time to take a computer course, which she hoped would improve her employment opportunities. She had also found a place to live within walking distance of the motel.

She was having other serious thoughts. Tomorrow her husband was being discharged from the Air Force, and he had already been admitted to

Clemson University. Should she go back to him? She caught her reflection in the mirror on the door and wondered if at twenty-five she wasn't a little old for college life. Who was she kidding? Air Force life had been impossible with its rules and regulations. She desperately needed open space. Yes, she had to make it on her own.

After Nancy smoothed the last bed, cleaned and restocked the bath and stuffed a pack of Mandarin matches in the pocket of her jeans, she stopped by the kitchen of the motel and ate a free meal. Then she began her walk home.

The sun was intense for late afternoon, and she put on her sunglasses as she walked. Soon a green 1973 Plymouth Satellite slowed down near her. The driver appeared to be about her own age. Music was coming through the open window as he stopped, smiled, and asked, "Do you want a ride?"

"Sure, why not?" Nancy replied and got into the car. She had always been gentle and trusting, and she truly believed that all people were basically good.

But she had never met anyone like Gerald Stano.

He was in a bad mood, but tried not to let it show. Jerry drifted into dark moods often, and this afternoon the reason was his forthcoming marriage in June. He could not believe that he had agreed to marry Mickey. She was such a bitch, but he did work for her father and breaking off wasn't going to be easy.

As he drove north on the beach, he listened to his chatty passenger. Nancy was talking about how materialistic the world was and how hard it was to make enough money for bare necessities like food. He nursed another beer and thought: *She's just like the others. She'll be coming on to me soon for money.*

"There should be more love in the world," she said, "and more understanding."

Love was what he had in mind, but not that kind of love. He loved his car, but he was confused by his lack of feelings for people. Others could have lasting personal relationships. Why couldn't he? He crossed over High Bridge going through Cobb's Corner to Old Dixie Highway. In Tomoka State Park, he turned on a narrow road used primarily by hunters. He stopped the car near some power lines.

"If you're tight on cash, I might be able to help you for some sex. You know, some money toward the rent," he said lasciviously. Nancy became furious. She was a warm person, but she needed some tenderness, and Jerry made no pretense of kindness. She demanded to be taken home.

She sounds just like Mickey, he thought. *Bitching, bitching, bitching. I don't take that from nobody.* He grasped Nancy's throat and shook her, tightening his fingers to cease her screaming.

"Damn you, be quiet," he screamed as her voice went from pitiful garbled sounds to silence. Even after her body went limp, he continued choking her. Sweating and salivating, he finally stopped his assault and pulled her body from the car. He laid her flat on her back in the middle of the road and drove to his parents' house in Ormond Beach.

The next morning, around eight o'clock, two teenage boys were hunting near a power line clearing just off a backwoods trail running north from Bulow Creek Road when they saw a woman's body lying in the dirt road. They carefully approached it as they would have an injured animal. The denim jacket and blue pullover blouse and bra were pulled up exposing her breasts, but there was no blood. Her blue jeans and blue bikini underwear were pulled down around her ankles, and the thighs were in a widespread position. Terror stricken, they ran back and called the Volusia County Sheriff's Office.

When detectives arrived, they found the Mandarin Motel matches and knapsack near the body. The ground was covered with dried weeds and twigs, which were undisturbed when the body had been placed there. There was no sign of a struggle.

Although Stano left the corpse configured as though he and the victim had been engaged in sexual activity, the medical examiner's report could not confirm that. Physical evidence is quickly lost as decomposition begins.

Nancy was traced to the hotel by the matches where her employer identified her. The murder remained unsolved until six years later when Gerald Stano confessed to strangling a blond maid from the Mandarin, described her and the death scene, and took police to the exact location where the body had been found.

Nine

The nude body of a pretty young woman washed up on the beach just south of Turtle Mound, and the newspaper headlines screamed, "DO YOU KNOW THIS GIRL?" Fishermen had found the nude body lying facedown half buried in the sand. She had apparently been dragged to the water and drowned. The small suntanned figure was wearing only a pair of gold earrings in her pierced ears.

In the summer of 1975, reports on runaways were routine. When the picture of this recently murdered girl was circulated, the number of heartbreaking calls was staggering: Is this my daughter, my sister, my friend?

There were numerous dead end calls and visits to the funeral home by people, some of whom had come long distances, hoping to put old worries to rest. The sixteen-year-old's body lay unclaimed for over a week. She was 115 pounds, five foot three inches tall with light brown hair and blue eyes. A bikini-style swimsuit had left its mark on her suntanned body. An upper front tooth was slightly chipped, and her short fingers had manicured nails. The young woman had been brutally beaten about the head and face.

Finally, the Sheriff's Office in New Smyrna Beach received a call from people in Flagler Beach who recognized the newspaper photograph. They went to the funeral home and confirmed the identity. This was Linda Ann Hamilton, a girl from Millbury, Massachusetts, who had been staying with them for awhile. They had seen her last on Monday, July 21, when she had left alone wearing only her bathing suit.

Linda said she was going to see a movie. Instead, she decided to walk the infamous beach amusement area.

Stano's green '73 Plymouth had already made several passes around the Loop. He kept his eye on Linda. He stopped the car, rolled down the window, and asked, "Do you want to ride and smoke a bit of herb?"

Linda didn't hesitate.

"Sure," she said as she slid into the passenger's seat. "This is a great car. Nice stereo, too."

Her remarks pleased Stano. He lit a joint for them to smoke and took off west over the Halifax River. As they left the carnival bright lights behind, she seemed nervous and started talking a lot.

"I'm just visiting," she offered. "My first trip to Florida. I like it okay, but I guess Spring Break is more interesting." She was hoping he would think she was in college.

Stano smiled and headed toward New Smyrna Beach. He had been married for exactly one month in what had already become a sexless marriage. Tonight would be different. He even felt happy as he headed south on A1A. He was going to score.

"This is Turtle Mound, an old Indian Burial ground," he said as he stopped the car. He had pulled the car to a point where you could see the ocean between the mounds of sea grapes and clumps of pampas grass. He popped a beer.

After a few minutes, Linda said, "I think I better get back. My friends will be worried. They expect me back after the movie."

"There's going to be a show," Jerry laughed, "just you and me."

"I don't think so," she shot back anxiously.

"Maybe I can convince you," he said as he punched her in the face. She cursed and struggled, but he had already ripped off her little bikini. When she kept moving, he started slapping her more. As he knew he would, he lost control and beat her almost to death.

"Why do you make me do this?" he cried, and squeezed his hands around her neck until her breathing stopped. After a few moments, he dragged her nude body out of the car and down the slope to the beach. He carefully turned her facedown in the damp sand and packed several inches of sand over her body. Tired, he stood over the body and masturbated in the moonlight.

He made his way back up the dune and tidied his car. He would get the sand out later. He wiped his forehead, opened another beer, and drove home. On his way home, he smiled. *Just another flirting bitch,* he thought. *Good riddance!*

When fishermen found the body the next day, the tide had washed the sand away. After she had been identified by her photograph, her parents flew down from Massachusetts. Sad and tired, they said that Linda had not contacted them for several weeks, and they did not know she was in Daytona Beach.

Linda Ann Hamilton's death remained a mystery until six years later when, on March 12, 1981, Gerald Stano confessed to the murder giving graphic details.

Ten

For Ramona Neal, tonight was the happiest, most exciting one she could remember. Forest Park, Georgia would never seem the same to her now that she had graduated from high school. The large, bustling house where her mom and dad had raised nine children, including herself and her twin brother, no longer seemed like a haven.

In her bedroom now, she heard the phone ring.

"It's me," her girlfriend said when Ramona jumped for the phone. "Well, it's official," she giggled.

"You got the reservations!" Ramona squealed. "Can't you see us now at the Mayan Inn, no less, all four of us living it up."

"I'm not sure where the others are staying . . . Holiday Inn, I think, and I really don't know how fifteen of us will fit in two cars,"

90

her friend was saying, "but I guess the guys will figure something out."

Ramona let all of her one hundred twenty-six pounds fall dead weight into her bean bag chair, laughing. "Maybe I'll get Dad to drive us all down in his truck."

The girls shrieked in unison, "I think the guys can figure something out." Then, "Talk to you later."

After hours of traveling, Ramona and her friends finally drove across the bridge to Daytona Beach, down Atlantic Avenue, and stopped at the Mayan Inn. The boys jumped out to help with the luggage, relieved to be getting rid of four passengers. Everyone was tired. The girls were all talking at once, making plans for tomorrow, except for Ramona who was quiet. Uncharacteristically, she and her boyfriend Bill had argued. She said a cool goodbye to him.

The next day, she put on her new blue polka dot bikini and joined her crowd on the beach.

The car traffic began to increase late in the afternoon. With twilight, the ocean calmed to a gentle roll of whitecaps to the beach. The pastel buildings along the Loop took on a different hue. People paired off, and some occupied the same sweater or blanket. The passing cars stopped to pick up single passengers, and prostitutes emerged to start their night's work.

She took the elevator up to Bill's room, but no one answered the door. Ramona was headed back to the picnic area just as a green '73 Plymouth Satellite Custom slowly cruised by her. Gerald Stano rolled down the tinted window, took a deep drag from the joint he was holding, and asked, "Want to get high with me, baby?"

Ramona said, "Why not?" and got into his car. They rode up the beach drinking beer and smoking pot. Jerry talked about his wife and their bad sex life. He turned the car west on Granada Avenue and crossed over the Halifax River on Ormond Bridge. The Shell station where he worked for his father-in-law was just three blocks ahead. There he turned north on Beach Street and headed for Tomoka Park. He complained about work tomorrow. Ramona didn't mind hearing about his personal life, but she was anxious to get back.

He could sense her apprehension, and he thought it would be fun to annoy her further by talking about historic sites in the area. He drove to the Bulow Plantation ruins in the park, where sugar mills and warehouses had been built out of native coquina rock. He told her the buildings were destroyed a long time ago in the Seminole Indian Wars.

"I don't like it out here," she complained nervously.

He turned off the lights and grabbed her, laughing. "I really didn't bring you out here for sight-seeing."

She was angry. "Is that the best you can do?" she asked.

Rage overcame Stano, and he grabbed her by the neck and strangled her to death. He dragged her body out of the car and dumped it into a ditch. He went back for a knife and stabbed her repeatedly to make sure she was dead. Carefully he crossed her arms and wiped his hands on her bikini. He covered her with weeds and branches and returned to the car. As he drove away, he turned up the stereo and said, "Son of a bitch! I've got to work tomorrow."

Three or four o'clock in the morning, he found his way home and parked abruptly beside the trailer. Exhausted, he stumbled out of the car; ignoring the lock, kicked open the metal door. His wife, Mickey, fully clothed, was struck motionless with horror when she saw his silhouette in the doorway. Her knees felt too weak to support her ample body, but she did not move. He staggered forward and a soft light from the bedroom cast an eerie glow. Terrified, she clasped both hands to her mouth to silence a scream when she saw that his clothes were saturated with blood. *My God,* she thought, *what has he done now?* His crazed eyes burned on her as if to say, don't ask.

Eleven

October 1978

Gerald Stano was riding around in the rain, desiring female company. This fall night was particularly slow, and he was getting frustrated. Bad weather left the beach empty except for a few die-hard walkers. There was no one on Atlantic Avenue or the Ocean Avenue Loop. He cruised by some of the motels but still saw nothing. He decided to check the bars so he eased the car to a stop on Main Street. From this spot he could observe both the Laundromat and Black Beard's Bar across the street.

He opened a beer, lit a cigarette and listened to the music. He liked to watch the rain bead up on the hood of his shiny red Gremlin. Main Street was also empty except for an occasional car, which he cursed as it spattered by him.

The rain formed patterns on the windshield and he thought about his old girlfriend, Claudia, back in Pennsylvania. *Damn her for marrying someone else.* Suddenly he saw her image in the raindrops. This vision had been occurring to him lately. She was always dressed in the blue velvet pantsuit that she wore on their first date. He could clearly see her long black hair and lips that moved saying nothing he could hear. He yelled her name, and sweat stood out on his forehead. The wipers slammed on. Now everything was clear again.

"Damn!" he hissed as he jerked out a Kleenex to wipe his thick glasses. At that moment a prostitute came out of the bar. She put her hands on her hips and surveyed the street traffic in both directions. Seeing only the Gremlin, she started moving toward Stano's car. He noticed how she walked in the red shorts and wondered how she could manage such high heels on the slippery street. She wore a dark T-shirt that said, "Do it in the Dark." He lowered the window, they made a deal, and she got into the car.

Jerry drove west across the bridge to US 1 and headed south. He was pleased with the company, liked the way she looked, but he didn't like the way she smelled. She wore cheap heavy perfume and she carried the damp odor from the rain. Before they had gone three blocks, she had refused a beer or cigarettes. Her mind was on her work, and she started talking to him about how he liked it. She reached over and rubbed his chest, undid his belt and pants, and started massaging him. Jerry could hardly keep the car on the road.

"Wait a minute until I park," he said breathlessly. She continued to fondle him, kissing his neck and ear. He pulled into a deserted parking lot and grabbed her.

"Wait a minute, honey. This is going to be great, but I need fifty bucks first," she smiled.

Stano became enraged. "Who cares what you need!" he screamed and slapped her face. He grunted and clutched her throat, squeezing hard. Soon she was silent. After she was dead, he had intercourse with her and propped her up on the front seat.

He drove slowly out of the parking lot and west to I-95. There were too many lights to dump the body so he turned south on the highway. He came to Taylor Road where the median strip between the divided highway was wooded. Sometimes highway patrol troopers sat here looking for drug dealers heading

Twelve

September 2, 1981

The bailiff shifted his weight from one foot to the other and coughed nervously. The extra security in the courtroom this morning for the big event meant the sheriff's deputies were tripping over each other. Gerald Stano was about to admit under oath that he had murdered six women, and he was going to be sentenced for three of those murders. Word travels fast in the courthouse, and everyone knew Stano's case was on Judge Foxman's docket. The spectator's gallery usually held one or two courthouse groupies, but today it was standing room only as people jammed in to get a close look at Daytona's serial killer.

The crowd stared as Stano was led from the holding cell connected to the courtroom. People along the back row craned their necks to see him. He was neatly dressed in a sport shirt and slacks. With his thinning hair and thick glasses, he looked like anyone you might meet on the street. Those who came to see a wild-eyed maniac were disappointed by his mild mannered appearance. He was handcuffed, and the manacles on his ankles were connected to the handcuffs by a heavy chain. As he was led into the room, they clanked. Several deputies hovered around Stano. The bailiffs were less concerned about an escape attempt than they were about the hostile crowd. Who knew if an angry father or boyfriend of one of his victims would try revenge?

Jerry was glad to see his attorney, Don Jacobson. This morning was the culmination of a plan conceived shortly after his arrest on April 1, 1980; a concerted effort by the defense team to keep him out of the electric chair. Jacobson smiled and shook Stano's nicotine stained hand, an awkward gesture due to the handcuffs. Jerry was a man of medium height, but he was much taller and heavier than the dapper lawyer. Jacobson looked tired, and his sixty-plus years showed through his thin smile.

Stano glanced over his shoulder and saw few friendly faces in the crowd. His parents and brother were there. They waved quickly, trying to preserve their anonymity. Suddenly he felt conspicuous, an oddity exhibited for public view.

The table for the defense attorney and the defendant was closest to the holding cell. A few feet away, closer to the judge's bench, was an identical table for the prosecutor. Assistant State Attorney Larry Nixon stood here arranging his notes and exhibits. Nixon had been a prosecutor for eight years, ever since graduating from law school. As he approached forty, his once long hair was graying and becoming thinner. His intense blue eyes never missed a thing going on around him. Everyone in the courthouse agreed that he was the best lawyer in the prosecutor's office. If some were put off by his brisk demeanor, they knew it was the impatience borne from his intelligence. He had been promoted quickly and now was the division chief responsible for every criminal prosecution occurring within the Daytona Beach city limits. Experience enabled him to retain a calm exterior, but inside he was excited about wrapping up the biggest case of his career.

A buzzer sounded and Judge James Foxman entered the courtroom. The bailiff intoned, "All rise. The Circuit Court in and for Volusia County, Florida, is now in session, the Honorable S. James Foxman presiding. All persons having business before this court, draw near and you shall be heard. May God save the United States of America, the State of Florida, and this honorable court. Be seated." The crowd shuffled to get resettled.

Judge Foxman had not been on the bench for many years, but he had already made a name for himself as a conscientious, thorough, and compassionate jurist. His attention to detail made him seem almost tedious, but it helped to keep him from being reversed on appeal. A widower with children, he was an impressive presence in his black robe, wire glasses, and neat haircut. This morning, his usually amiable expression reflected the seriousness of the occasion. He called the court to order.

"This case is the State of Florida versus Gerald Eugene Stano; there are three cases. Let the record reflect that Mr. Stano is here in person; he's represented by Don Jacobson out of Daytona Beach; Larry Nixon represents the State of Florida. Gentlemen, the first matter that we're here on this morning is a Motion for Determination of Competency of the Defendant to Stand Trial. I've received reports of five psychiatrists, Dr. Davis, Dr. Stern, Dr. Carrera, Dr. Barnard, and Dr. Ann McMillan. I would propose at this time, gentlemen, that I receive a stipulation and we stipulate the reports of the psychiatrists into evidence."

The prosecutor agreed with the stipulation. Every doctor who examined Stano had found him to be competent to stand trial; the only disagreement among the doctors was his sanity at the time the offenses were committed. Mr. Jacobson noted that he had requested the evaluations in the first place and so also stipulated to their admission. Based on the unanimous reports, the judge found Stano competent to stand trial. So far, no surprises. These intricate movements were well orchestrated; this courtroom dance was familiar as all the steps were choreographed in advance.

Nixon's turn came next. He outlined for the court the agreement that it had taken so many months to resolve. Stano would plead guilty to the murders of Mary Carol Maher, Toni Van Haddocks, and Nancy Heard. Three other cases were offered as similar fact evidence, but no formal charges were filed in those. Linda Hamilton, Ramona Neal, and Jane Doe (the unidentified prostitute) were finally laid to rest as Stano admitted killing these girls. Donna Hensley, the prostitute who was responsible for apprehending this serial killer, would never have to face him again because the state dropped the aggravated battery charge as part of the plea bargain. In view of the fact that Stano's parole eligibility date would not come up until he was over one hundred years old, the state dismissed the case to expedite his trip to the state prison in Starke.

The plea agreement was in writing. Nevertheless, Judge Foxman carefully reviewed the agreement with Stano. In exchange for his pleas of guilty in the Maher, Van Haddocks, and Heard cases, the State agreed not to prosecute the Hensley, Hamilton, Neal, and Doe cases, and further agreed that Stano would not receive a sentence of death. The only possible sentences under Florida law upon conviction of first-degree murder are death or life in prison with no parole for at least twenty-five years. During the prison term, no time for good behavior is deducted; the murderer serves twenty-five calendar years before becoming eligible for parole. Today the judge was sentencing Stano for three homicides. The court had the option of running the three sentences concurrently or stacking the twenty-five year terms consecutively. The court explained these options, and Stano stated that he understood.

"Other than that, there is no other plea agreement. Agreed, Mr. Stano?" said the judge.

"Yes, sir," replied Jerry.

Stano was placed under oath and the judge went through the formal colloquy necessary to accept a guilty plea. All of the constitutional rights waived by entry of a guilty plea were explained: the right to jury trial, the right to silence, the right to cross-examine the State's witnesses, and the severe limitation on the right to appeal mistakes. Stano stated under oath that he understood these rights and had fully discussed them with Jacobson, and that he was fully satisfied with his lawyer's services. Jacobson agreed, "We've spent many hours together going over this in detail. We've discussed the possibility of going to trial with the lid off as far as the electric chair. The decision has been Mr. Stano's, not Don Jacobson's. Isn't that right, Jerry?"

"Yes, sir," confirmed Stano.

"Anybody forcing you to plea or twisting your arm?" the judge inquired.

"No, sir," answered Jerry.

The prosecutor related the facts of the three homicides as a factual basis for the pleas. Nixon explained what the State would have proved had Stano gone to trial.

Before imposing sentence, Judge Foxman asked Stano if he had anything to say. He asked to have a few words with his parents and brother in the courtroom, one last conversation with his immediate family before being branded a murderer. The judge complied with this request. After a brief recess, Judge Foxman imposed sentence.

"Mr. Stano," said Judge Foxman, "the information before me, these three cases, lead me to believe that the death sentence may very well have been appropriate in any of those three cases. Perhaps all of them. I reluctantly agreed not to sentence you to death, to eliminate the possibility of the death penalty, because you have disclosed information that has provided families that didn't know where their loved ones were. With at least the information or the knowledge of where they are, this information put some of their traumas to rest. And, simply because of that, I have agreed to eliminate the possibility of a death sentence in this case. My conscience bothers me. I think that in these three cases, the death sentence would be probably appropriate. In essence, you profited simply because of the large number of murders you have committed.

"Mr. Stano, it is the intent of this Court that you shall not walk the streets of this state again as a free man. You shall serve a minimum of 75 years in prison before parole eligibility."

The deputies escorted Stano back to the holding cell. The audience slowly dispersed. Everyone involved thought that this was the last time the world would hear from Gerald Eugene Stano.

Thirteen

September 1981-June 1982

Stano felt very alone in the Volusia County Jail. For the first time since his confession to the Maher murder seventeen months ago, he had nothing to look forward to, nothing to base hopes on. There were no more doctors' evaluations, no more question sessions with Paul Crow to solve old cases, no lawyers' letters or telephone calls to discuss his cases and possible sentences, no planned family visits to give him strength and support. Owing to lack of funds, Don Jacobson was no longer representing Stano officially. Jerry had been convicted of murdering six women, but had escaped the electric chair.

After all of the delays, all of the waiting, all of the continuances, the court hearing was over so quickly that Stano could hardly believe it. He would be in jail the rest of his life. Everyone knew about the other Jerry now, the murderer of six women.

So far jail really had not been that bad. He had been well-treated there during his questioning. Jerry had his stereo, books to read, and a television set. He wasn't sure what to expect at Florida State Prison. Although he had visited several State locations during his psychological examinations and tours of the state, he had never been to the prison which would be his new home.

Until Judge Foxman's sentence, Jerry and his family could ignore or rationalize his crimes. Now he was a murderer, and five doctors had examined him and eliminated mental illness as an excuse or an avenue to a reduced sentence. In the past, his family had always glossed over his problems by changing schools or relocating to a new town. Jerry had continued the pattern all his life. Wherever he encountered anyone who questioned his lying, stealing or the other Jerry's antisocial behavior, he simply moved on.

Jerry loved the notoriety of his status as a confessed serial killer. The newspaper articles and television coverage made him feel important, like a celebrity. People recognized him. At the hearing there was a large crowd, and he even remembered seeing movie cameras.

The guards told Jerry that the request for his pickup by the Florida State Prison had been sent to Starke. There had been a lot in the newspapers and television news about the prison system during the last two or three years, and most of it was bad. Overcrowding, homosexual rape, and inmate riots over bad conditions made him wonder. The State had claimed improvements. Jerry hoped that they were true reports. He would know soon.

Jerry had always loved to ride in a car. Even in the back of the State Prison white van, sitting in leg irons and hand irons looking out through the small diamonds of heavy gauge wire, he still didn't mind the ride. He could almost describe the route and road scenes with his eyes shut. The one-hundred-plus-mile trip from DeLand started north on Highway 17. He remembered that the road featured gentle hills and a variety of signs referring to Lake George on the left and Crescent Lake on the right. A series of little towns with three and four businesses dotted the route. DeLeon Springs, Barberville, Pierson, Seville, Crescent City, Pamona Park, Satsuma and San Mateo were all familiar to Jerry. One town was the turnoff to the Ocala National Forest. Another was a farm worker town, and others boasted the sale of ferns and houseplants. Crescent City, which is a little larger than the rest, claimed to be the area's bass fishing capital. Jerry remembered fishing as a boy with his grandfather. *No more fishing now,* he thought.

When he saw a two- or three-mile stretch of stores and businesses, Jerry knew that they were reaching East Palatka and the St. Johns River. The river widens at Palatka and the high bridge gives a good view of the town and river. Jerry tried for the second or third time to get the guards to talk, but they were not interested.

Palatka was alive with activity. Jerry noticed the large number of young people on the street and thought of the community college on the far side of town. He remembered the college was on the road to Gainesville, a pretty, winding road going due west through the town of Hawthorne. Two girls in the rain and a white church flashed through his mind.

Today the route from Palatka was State Road 100 northwest to Starke. Flat, desolate land with an occasional pulp mill or power plant passed by. After another hour of small towns they reached Starke. Jerry knew that his natural parents had obtained their wedding license in Starke. Odd that he should be coming here as a permanent resident. He remembered a visit eight years ago when he had driven through Starke just after he left a girl's body in a landfill.

Starke was still small and boring. They headed out of town on State Road 16. There were large farms and cows in the fields. Finally, Jerry saw some isolated pale green buildings on a flat plane in the distance. As they drew closer, he could see two parallel fences over twenty feet apart surrounding the buildings. The fences were topped with curled barbed wire. He guessed one fence was at least eight feet and the other about ten feet tall. Jerry asked the guard their actual height and he answered, "Tall enough!"

They slowed down for a gate. When the van faced the gate, Jerry saw a plain metal arch with block letters which read, "State Prison." He noticed guard dogs between the two rows of fence.

A brown-shirted guard in a gun tower at the entrance gate demanded to know their business. The driver reported that a prisoner was being delivered. The guard called the administration office to confirm the delivery and opened the outer metal gate electronically. The van moved forward to a position between the gates. The outer was closed behind them, clanking as it jarred along the track. In all,

Jerry counted five electric gates or doors and metal detectors before they reached the processing area of the Central Administration Building.

He went through the intake process quickly. Picture, number 079701, cell L-2-N-5, blue uniform, job assignment, briefing on rules and routine. He learned about metal trays, plastic forks and spoons, and single rooms to prevent homosexual rape. All of this information was imparted briskly and loudly. When he tried to make small talk he was quickly silenced. He was informed that just six months ago there were two and one half times as many people here. How lucky he was to be here now with a population under the maximum designed for the building.

Jerry was quickly made aware of the unofficial hierarchy as well as the official organization. The prison authorities explained that blue uniforms were for ordinary prisoners like him and orange T-shirts were for Death Row inmates. Normal term inmates were in two wings, one where he was assigned and the other for the mentally unstable. A separate wing was reserved for the Death Row inmates.

What they had not explained was that the notoriety of inmates was determined not by

112

the seriousness of their crime but by the death sentence and the publicity their trial received. Jerry had admitted killing six women, been on television and in newspapers. But because of his mere life sentence he was a second-echelon inmate in prison. He was issued a blue shirt. The attention and respect Jerry expected was not forthcoming, and he was unhappy. Soon he would pine for the extra privileges Death Row inmates enjoyed like television sets and stereos in their cell.

Ted Bundy, killer of two Florida State sorority sisters and a Lake City schoolgirl, was an attractive and articulate Death Row celebrity. Florida's Death Row had many notorious inmates, so many that the guards joked that soon they would have to install electric bleachers. Jerry did not fit in again. He had been convicted of killing twice as many women as Bundy, but he was not receiving his kind of recognition.

Stano had no choice but to fit into the flow at Florida State Prison. Even though he was kept busy, he had a lot of time to think about his situation.

Other people were still thinking about him, too. Paul Crow was convinced that Jerry knew more than he had admitted thus far. During his last group of murder confessions in March, Jerry slipped and included details of another unsolved case of a body found near Titusville in another jurisdiction. Crow could never get him to talk about that case again. It was set aside and the prosecution was made on the six confessed murders.

The publicity of the multiple murder conviction had attracted the attention of other police agencies. Many called or wrote to Paul Crow asking for assistance in possibly closing unsolved cases with data from Gerald Stano. Paul Crow contacted Jerry at the prison in the fall of 1981 and early 1982 trying to clear up open cases. He was also visited and questioned without result by Sheriff's deputies from Titusville and Gainesville in early 1982.

Jerry's options were limited as he viewed them. Five doctors had repeatedly declared him sane and fit to stand trial. Jerry certainly wanted to avoid being labeled a "roasty toasty" like the inmates in S wing, the section of FSP reserved for the criminally insane. They were housed in cells with no furniture and few clothes. Jerry was smarter than that, and no one would try to be there on purpose. Judge Foxman's sentence would keep Jerry in jail without parole past his hundredth birthday. Release was no option either. Here there was no notoriety, no interviews, no special attention or special treatment. He was not on Death Row. His boasting fell on deaf ears.

Jerry tried the usual avenues prisoners explore to change their fate. In January 1982, he wrote to Don Jacobson requesting $500 to finance a sure transfer scheme through a fellow inmate. In February, he requested through his lawyer a transfer to the maximum security facility being built on Indian Lake Road in Volusia County. He asked if his sentence could be changed from twenty-five years mandatory minimum without parole to twelve years for each of the three.

Jerry had been thinking about his situation for nine months. He remembered how he was the star, the center of attraction at the Volusia County Jail. Paul Crow and Don Jacobson had taken care of him. They met his demands for comfort. He avoided the electric chair when he really deserved it. Judge Foxman even said so. Jerry decided that he could again be the center of attraction and gain more status and creature comforts in prison by cooperating with Paul Crow. On Death Row he could get a stereo, a personal television set, wear an orange shirt, and be a big name. If he had to spend the rest of his life in prison anyway, he thought he had better do something to move himself up in the unofficial prison hierarchy. Jerry had nothing to

115

lose. The thrill of confession replaced the thrill of murdering. The status and comforts in confinement meant more to him than the threat of the electric chair. The media attention was important too because, in his mind, it raised him above the crowds. He was no ordinary murderer. Jerry was a bona fide serial killer.

On June 6, 1982, Stano wrote Paul Crow this letter:

Paul Crow —
    Hello,
    I want to write you at this time to tell you that *when ever you want me to take that drug,* (Truth drug) *you can do it.* But it must be done in the County jail. *Also, my parents are to be left out of this and also my brother and his family.*

    I would expect the following:
    1. 1 man cell at VCJ.
    2. Legal counsel from a Public Defender.
    3. Notarized papers stating what will be done and that it will be done at the Volusia County Jail.
    4. Phone calls to the family when I arrive at the County Jail.

5. *Paul Crow* will escort me to the Volusia County Jail *or* the Volusia County Sheriff's Department. Paul, this must be *kept out* of the papers. While this is [taken] place, you may have the other man you said was up to see me there also.

Please *get back in touch with me as soon as possible about this. Because I would like to clear up your files for you.*

Paul, please realize where I am coming from. *I will help you, if you help me. By that I mean by telling you what you want to know about anything.* I think about things up here. Please, Paul, listen to me this time as you have done before.

I will be waiting for a reply to my letter as soon as possible. *But I must have legal counsel and my parents are to be left out of this.*

Respectfully,
Jerry

P.S. My address is on the envelope.

When Paul Crow received this letter, he

read it and reread it, then pushed back his chair to think. He had waited for this break for a long time. Crow already had spent so many hours playing Jerry's games of cat and mouse that he had almost given up hope. Stano admitted committing four to six murders a year for seven years. Paul Crow wondered about the actual count. Who were the victims? Where are they? Whose vigil for a missing daughter or sister would end? Crow decided to accept Stano's offer. He notified Larry Nixon at the State Attorney's office of his request to arrange the transfer through Judge Foxman.

A few days after the letter was written to Paul Crow, Stano was summoned to Col. T.L. Barton's office at FSP where he was strip searched. Although he was told that they were searching for currency, which is contraband in prison, his clothes were kept in a plastic bag. Later he was told by a worker that his clothes were sent to the FBI.

Jerry reported all of this to Don Jacobson by letter on June 24, 1982. Jacobson answered on July 12, and offered a possible explanation for the strip search. He advised Jerry to tell all he knew. He reminded him that his immunity deal with the state no longer existed, and he suggested that Paul Crow was the best source for future deals.

On August 5, 1982, Judge Foxman entered an order transferring Stano from FSP to Volusia County Jail, until he completed his cooperation in the new investigation. Stano was picked up at Florida State Prison a few days later and brought back home. Paul Crow tightly controlled Stano and restricted access to him as he requested.

On Wednesday, August 11, Crow began a period of extensive interrogations of Stano. Since the open cases that fit the Stano pattern were in other nearby police jurisdictions, Crow was replaced in the questioning and taped confession sessions by other police department representatives. They all wanted to he sure that Jerry was telling the facts as he knew them and not simply parroting information which had been fed to him by Crow or someone else. No one wanted to be responsible for tainting a big case like this by shoddy police work. Crow was not informed of the details of the crimes by the other police agencies.

During one visit, Jerry was hypnotized by a local hypnotist hired by law enforcement officials. Crow's notes indicate that the session was not helpful. ". . . took GES back to six years old. No benefit from session. Resisted about homicides." Jerry got stuck in his childhood and cried about his memories of parental discipline. He did not progress past his early teenage years. When asked during hypnosis to think of a happy time as a child, Jerry described how he had once strangled a chicken. Those present wondered if this was the first time he got pleasure from killing something.

Even with this nonproductive session, by August 15, Jerry had confessed to five additional murders. Since these murders involved four different jurisdictions, the confessions were announced by the different agencies involved.

Donald Denton, from the Bradford County Sheriff's Department, taped Stano's confession to the Barbara Bauer murder. Johnny Manis, a Brevard County detective, taped the Sandra DuBose and Cathy Lee Scharf confessions. Dave Hudson, a Volusia County Sheriff's deputy, obtained the Susan Bickrest confession tape and a Hillsborough County detective questioned Stano about the Dorothy Williams murder.

1973 Barbara Bauer
1973 Cathy Scharf
1975 Susan Bickrest

1978 Sandra DuBose
1979 Dorothy Williams

Gerald Stano was returned to Florida State Prison on August 17, 1982.

Fourteen

September 6, 1973

The Bauer family sat around the breakfast table where the smells of many home cooked meals seasoned the room. The kitchen had always been where the family began and ended the day talking about news that interested them.

This September morning, Mrs. Bauer had a lot to say about the beginning of school. Though certainly not a novelty to her by now, teaching third grade was always a challenge. She looked across the table at her daughter, Barbara. It was hard to believe that the twins were actually about to begin their senior year at New Smyrna High School. It seemed only yesterday that they walked hand-in-hand to the first grade.

"Mom," she said, patting her hand, "I'm going to love this year. Cheerleading is so much fun and the dance is coming up. I'll look like a different person now that my braces are finally off." She wore her curly brown hair short, giving her a look of action. Whatever was going on this year she'd try to be an integral part of it. "I'm going to pick up material for my uniform at Holly Hill today. I can't wait to get started on it."

Her brother's eyes danced as he flashed a broad smile. They both shared wholesome good looks. "Just what Mom needs," he teased, "another project."

"At least the horses don't need fancy dressing," Dr. Bauer, their father, said. As a veterinarian, many of the horses he treated were owned by little girls. Few of them had his daughter's curiosity and zest for life, he thought. Barbara was never afraid to try something new, and she learned quickly. He was proud that she was an honor student in school. He had a lot of good memories like teaching her to roller skate on the wooden floors in the living room. His wife had been a good sport over the years. There were always two cakes for the twins' birthday, and everybody got equal time. He shared much with his son, but that was men's stuff. When the family went to the Grand Canyon, he had hiked to the bottom of the gorge with his boy. He smiled as he thought of how jealous Barbara had been not to be included on the hike.

Hopefully, next year she could go along.

Her brother glanced at his watch and jumped up from the table. "I've got to hurry." He gave his mother a little hug. "See you about 5:30." To his sister he said, "See you for dinner. You're taking the car today, right?"

"Yes," she answered. "I've got to go shopping, remember?"

Shortly after her brother left, Barbara kissed her father on the cheek and waved goodbye to her mother.

With her shopping done, Barbara returned to the parking lot, turned on her car's ignition, and discovered a dead battery. She decided to call her father. At this moment, Gerald Stano drove up beside her in his identical 1973 Plymouth Duster and volunteered his help. He had been fired from the Burroughs Corporation in Paoli, Pennsylvania and had just arrived in Florida. He had thought shopping for car tapes would cheer him up. That could wait. The coincidence of the identical cars interested him now.

"What's wrong," he asked cheerfully as he got out of his car. "Car won't start? Let me take a look." She gratefully agreed. He had cables in his trunk and quickly started her engine. "I think we should take it for a test ride to make sure the battery is charged," he suggested.

"Hey, that's nice of you," she said as she climbed into her car beside him. She had appreciated his help but as the test ride got longer, she got nervous. His conversation was entirely about their cars.

"She is different from this one. No automatic transmission, but did you notice the Avenger 60s and slotted disc mags? She has three speed on the column and a beautiful stereo system. Her behind is raised because of the air shocks."

"I want to go back," Barbara announced.

Her lack of interest infuriated him. He hit her with the back of his hand. She screamed in pain. "Please take me back," she begged again.

He was beginning to enjoy her misery. "If you do what I say, you won't get hurt," he lied. They rode on. He became confused about where he was and the scenery along the road looked unfamiliar. She was still sobbing which made him angry again, and he stopped the car. He grabbed her by the throat and choked her until she passed out. She regained consciousness to plead with him not to kill her. He choked her until she passed out again.

He continued his journey. It was beginning to get dark. Down the road he saw a filling station, and noted his empty gas tank. Before stopping at the station, he pulled over and warned his terrified passenger to keep quiet or he would kill her. She began to scream uncontrollably, and he choked her again until she was silent. He drove to a tank away from the attendant's view to pump the gas.

Back on the road again, Barbara regained consciousness and began to ramble incoherently. She was in dreadful pain and frightened out of her mind. Her babbling infuriated Stano. He turned down a dirt road and violently grasped her throat again. This time he killed her.

It was almost twilight. He tied her hands and feet with a venetian blind cord he found. He carried her from the car and laid her carefully in a small ditch. There was a dumpsite nearby with evidence of a busy day, but tonight it was completely vacant. Stano stood over her and played with her body. He undid her cutoff jeans but did not remove them. He poked at her little breasts and tugged at her T-shirt. He spat on her and masturbated himself to climax. Tiring of his macabre game, he returned to the car and started driving north on Interstate 75. He was returning to Pennsylvania, but, when his mind cleared, he realized that the car he was driving belonged to Barbara.

His singular purpose now was to get rid of the car and get back to the Holly Hill Plaza where his own car was parked. As he approached Valdosta, Georgia, he saw a lighted motel sign off the interstate. He immediately pulled into the motel, drove around back, and parked Barbara's car. He tossed the keys into the backseat and they landed on her previously purchased package of material that would now never be sewn. He pulled out a piece of fabric and wiped the car for prints. Finished, he tossed the cloth in the backseat and locked the car.

He saw an empty cardboard box and tore it for a sign on which he printed, "FLA." Back to the interstate, he soon got a ride back to Daytona and then another ride to his car. It was almost morning now, and he was completely exhausted from the night's activities. He checked into a beach motel and slept before driving back to Norristown.

When Barbara did not return home for dinner, her family became worried and called the police. Their fears grew daily; as the weeks and months passed, all hope disappeared. Her mother desperately sent letters to police agencies throughout Florida describing her daughter. Her father searched frantically for Barbara himself. They sought psychic advice, exploring any possibility for news, but to no avail.

Seven agonizing months later, Barbara's body was found near a landfill about one hundred miles from her home. Dental records confirmed the identification. Grief for their loss still lingers in the Bauer household. There are sleepless nights, guilt trips, and thoughts of vengeance. Her twin brother received his high school diploma on a stage without her. When he got married, she was not there to walk down the aisle with him. On birthdays now there is only one cake.

Fifteen

"Bye, Mom!" In one fluid motion, Cathy Lee Scharf bolted out the front door to her Port Orange home, and jumped over the porch steps, her long blond hair flying. She slid into her denim jacket on this chilly evening and jogged down the driveway eager to meet the night. It was just a few days until Christmas vacation, and this pretty seventeen-year-old high school student should have been studying. Cathy Lee had other plans. She met two girlfriends, Mary Jane and Amy, at the end of the driveway, and she hopped into their car.

They all wore blue jeans, rings and Indian jewelry, no makeup and long hair parted in the middle in the uniform of the times. But few could pull off the natural look as well as Cathy. She was a beauty. Her large blue eyes took in everything. Her good looks opened many doors to Daytona's wild nightlife.

The trio hit a few local bars in a marathon party that lasted all night. Each time they left a bar to go somewhere else, the group grew in number. Some people the girls knew before, others were new.

About three in the morning, Cathy suddenly realized that Amy and Mary Jane had gone off and she had no ride home. She stayed at another friend's house and slept a few hours until morning.

When she woke up, everything seemed confusing and unfamiliar. She straightened herself in the brisk morning air and started hitchhiking home. She got a ride over to the mainland, back to U.S. 1. She got out and started thumbing again as she walked south toward Port Orange.

As fate would have it, Stano was driving this same route looking for sex when he spied Cathy along the side of the road. He thought she looked pretty good for a hooker. He stopped his new green Plymouth Satellite, they smiled a greeting, and she got in.

Their relationship went downhill from that moment. Stano had been drinking heavily, and she was tired of partying. She wanted to eat breakfast, but he didn't. Sex was the only thing on his mind. He turned and tried to kiss her, but she pushed him away.

"All I want is a ride," she said firmly.

"Aw, come on," he laughed, groping at her. "This ride isn't free."

"Take your hands off of me," she shouted. "You're gross!"

When she said that, Stano hit her. She was angry and yelling and tried to get out the door. He was delighted with her misery. He slapped her again. "Those locks are burglar proof, you can't get them open," he sneered. He turned off U.S. 1 and headed for the northern edge of Merritt Island.

"Where in the hell are we," Cathy asked, coming out of a daze. "I live the other way in Port Orange," she cried. "Let me out of here! Slow down, damn you!" She tried to open the door again to jump out but could not. She turned and struck him, cutting his cheek with her Indian-head ring.

Enraged and excited, he stopped the car and choked her until she passed out.

He was cruising now, driving fast toward the beach side. He came to a dirt road which led through a citrus grove, and there he stopped about fifty feet from a dark canal. He did not want to scratch his car. He looked at her and she was awake again, her blue eyes wide with terror. The finality of his next statement made her catch her breath.

"This is the end of the line," he said.

She started shaking and crying. *The fight's out of her now,* he thought. He went into his ritual of stabbing her with superficial wounds, then choking her until she passed out. He knew just how long to strangle her so that she would just pass out and not die. He waited until her body went limp, then he would let go and let her come back to life. She begged him to let her go each time she came to consciousness, but he laughed and enjoyed his cruel game. He prolonged the enjoyment of killing her for hours. Finally, she didn't awake; she was dead.

For a while he stared at her, sweating, softly swearing. When his pulse rate slowed, he picked Cathy's body up and started carrying it through the mud to the canal. A light rain began to fall. It felt good on his face. He laid her body down on the bank and covered it with palm branches. Satisfied with a neat job, he drove back to a service station to wash his hands and face. He combed his hair and cleaned the mud from his shoes. He decided that roller skating would be a fun way to end the morning. On his way to the skating rink, he discovered Cathy's purse in his car and threw the wallet into the river.

When Cathy did not return home, her mother contacted the police. They, with some of Cathy's friends, traced the events of the night before. The trail stopped when Cathy began to hitchhike home.

On January 19, 1974, about a month later, two men were hunting wild hogs near Haulover Canal in Brevard County. Deep in the thick woods, they smelled the odor of something rotting. Soon they found Cathy's decomposing body covered with palmetto fronds. Horrified, they drove to the canal tender to report their discovery.

Soon the authorities arrived at the grisly scene. Her feet and legs were on the bank of the ditch. Her head and shoulders were in the murky water. An area of skin was gone and the ribs were exposed beneath her shirt, which was pulled up around her shoulders. The side of her body was stained with dried blood. She was only thirty miles from home.

Experts concluded that the death had been a ritualistic murder, due to the large amount of blood and also because of the unusual positioning of the body. The calves were folded underneath her thighs toward the sides. From the Indian jewelry, the clothing, and her teeth, the police were able to make a positive identification. Later, two small boys who were fishing between Port Orange and New Smyrna Beach found a wallet which Mrs. Scharf identified as Cathy's.

The murder was unsolved until August 11, 1982, when a homicide investigator with the Brevard County Sheriff's Office, Johnny Manis, taped a confession from Stano. Stano described the victim's appearance, where he took her, and how he had killed her. All of these details confirmed the earlier reports on her death. Stano showed no remorse for the killing for which he probably will be electrocuted. He described how he repeatedly strangled her into unconsciousness only to let her awake and relive the horrible nightmare. He took several hours torturing Cathy before he finally killed her. He said that in order to kill someone in such a prolonged manner, "You've got to pace yourself."

Sixteen

December 20, 1975

P.J.'s had been packed all evening. The beachside bar was always smoky and smelled of stale beer, but after fifteen weeks of working here, Susan Bickrest was getting the hang of it. She had learned to get her orders straight over the loud rock music and to deliver them back to the table with the kind of walk that said she expected a tip. The customers were lively, and their conversations were sometimes punctuated with waving beer bottles. She had met a lot of guys there and had gone out with some of them after work.

She brightened considerably when she saw one of her friends, Joe, sitting at the bar nursing a beer. He was waiting for closing time so he could be with her. He watched her intently. They had already been on several dates during the weeks since they met, and he had enjoyed her company. Tonight, Joe had been Christmas shopping with another girlfriend, Nancy, for several hours. He was tired. He had taken Nancy and her daughter home, had a shower, and borrowed her car to come here to find Susan.

Susan nodded a greeting from across the room. After a while, she set an empty tray down on the bar next to his stool. As he turned his stool, he opened his knees to hold her captive for a moment. The crowd was beginning to lessen. She laughed and said, "It's only about fifteen minutes until closing time. Think you can wait?" She wiggled free.

"How about some breakfast?" he asked sheepishly.

"You're on," she smiled. "Where?"

"How about Sambo's?"

"You drive on over, and I'll meet you there. I have a little work left here."

"That's fine, Susan," he said, and left in Nancy's car.

A short time later Susan parked her car at Sambo's, went directly to the back of the restaurant where Joe and some other friends were about to order. They ate for almost an hour, laughing and talking. Afterwards in the parking lot outside, Joe announced that he was tired and was going home. Disappointed, Susan started her Camaro and Joe drove behind her across the Broadway Bridge. Susan made the green light at Second Avenue and drove west. Joe turned north when his light changed.

It was nearly closing time when Stano left P.J.'s lounge. He cruised around and drank a six-pack of beer. He had seen Susan leave the lounge in her white Camaro. He always noticed the cars as much as the girls. He admired her light sandy hair and the black top on her car. Just as he was thinking that he'd like to see her again, her white Camaro whisked by him in the rain, and he stalked it from a distance.

Susan arrived at her apartment and locked up her car. There were few cars moving about at this hour. A haze blew in from the ocean and made an eerie glow from the headlights. She noticed this light distortion as Jerry Stano's car whipped into the parking spot next to her.

"I need somebody to talk to. How about you?" he inquired, trying to sound engaging. He opened his car door for her. "Think you would enjoy a ride and some conversation?"

"I really don't think so." She tried to sound final.

"Sure you do," he insisted, and pointed a small caliber gun at her.

She was very frightened, but thought it would be best to do what he demanded. She thought her chances of survival were better if she cooperated. She slipped into his car.

"Get some life in you, girl," Jerry laughed, after a short while thoroughly enjoying himself. "We're going to have a good old time."

"Take me home," she pleaded. Her face was flushed. "Who in the hell do you think you are? I have a friend on the police force, you know."

Anger swelled in his face. He spat at her and hit her hard across the jaw. His ring cut her cheek, and the blood excited him.

"Oh my God!" she cried and shook with uncontrollable tears.

"Bitch!" he yelled, and hit her again. He continued driving south on I-95. He could see in the minimal light that he had messed up her face, and it had begun to swell. *Ugly bitch,* he thought, as he stopped the car to take a leak.

Jerry hoped this one would give him a chase. He got off better after the physical exertion. Jerry's eyes popped in demonic glee. Sweat beaded up on his brow, and his mouth twisted into a leer. *This one has some life in her after all.* He was excited. A good chase was Jerry's foreplay.

He easily caught her and slapped her down. She kicked and screamed as he pounded her into unconsciousness. This time he picked her limp body up and placed her on the front seat. He locked the doors and drove down the highway until he exited at Taylor Road in Port Orange. He took the first left onto Airport Road, an unpaved street that skirted the Spruce Creek Fly-In, an old military training base that had been turned into a swanky development. As he turned down the road, his lights danced off the thick palmetto growth. In this remote area at the head of Spruce Creek, he parked the car, turned off the lights, and waited for Susan to wake up.

When she startled into consciousness, he tortured her some more, hitting and strangling her. Faint moonlight peeping through the dark clouds allowed him to see her battered face and bloody leather jacket. He tumbled out of the car and felt sandy marsh under his feet. He dropped to his knees and splashed water on his face. Refreshed, he returned to the car and hoped that Susan would be awake again for more fun and games. He brushed her blond hair away from her disfigured face, to find that she was dead.

Jerry carried her body across the sand and threw her into the shallow water. One of her shoes fell by the bank of the creek. Washing his hands once again, he returned to his car. He got in, turned the car around, and headed back to the highway. Christmas music was on the radio, and he quickly switched stations. *It's really late,* he thought. *Good thing my wife is at her mother's tonight.*

At about 4:40 that afternoon, two men were fishing on Spruce Creek, about a half mile west of Moody Bridge when they saw a figure floating in the water. At first they thought it was a mannequin. When they discovered it was a human body, they hurried to a nearby gas station to call the sheriff.

By the time investigators arrived, the tide

140

had carried the body out of view. They got into the boat and started the search. When they found the body and got it in the boat, the corpse was stiff, with arms extending straight out from floating facedown. On her right hand she still wore a silver opal ring, a gift from a Christmas past.

Seventeen

August 1978

Usually it's fun to hear "Happy Birthday" sung, even off-key, but the irony of this particular rendition was that it was being directed at Sandra DuBose, a confused person who had seen precious few happy days of any kind in her thirty-five years. She had been born blind, and although expensive operations had restored partial vision, she was now going blind again. She could barely see the single candle flickering on the cake in front of her.

It was not just from lack of vision, however. She had been drinking heavily for hours at various beachside dives, ending up here at the Booby Trap, perhaps the sleaziest of them all. It was only because she was a regular that anyone knew it was her birthday. The pathetic collection of barflies were Sandra's only friends.

The brief moment of recognition passed, the singing trailed away, and the candle went out. Someone bought Sandra another drink. She was pleased with the company when Jerry Stano sat down on the empty seat beside her.

Over the years the alcohol abuse had made her overweight, but she kept her hair neat and her complexion good. She also liked to talk.

Jerry had been drinking himself and was equally pleased to have some company. "Is the birthday girl from around here?" he asked pleasantly, not bothering to get her name straight.

"Yes. Cocoa," she replied and then commenced to give him her life story. He was fascinated with details which seemed to parallel some of his own life. She had been sexually molested as a young girl and had spent much of her life in psychiatric care. He knew about those kind of doctors.

"Yeah, I know about those quacks," Jerry said. "We had to go to a marriage counselor, but all those guys want to do is fuck your wife," he said tersely. "What jerks. It'd be easy to fake being nuts. Those doctors are all blockheads."

"Who's faking?" she laughed and drained her glass. She motioned for another. "My life was messed up good. Forever, I guess. What's your problem?" she asked.

"I think my troubles started back in Pennsylvania, where I'm from," he said. "My girlfriend's father threatened me with a gun. I got her pregnant and she had to get an abortion. That is when I started drinking to forget. It was the beginning of the end for me." He was surprised that he could talk to someone this candidly. Sometimes two strangers can discuss things that neither would normally utter to friends or family.

"I can't remember when I didn't need booze," Sandra confided, looking down at the ice in her near empty glass. She brightened. "How's your love life, honey? Let's talk about love."

Jerry remembered someone else in his life who was sick and said, "I rarely drank until I moved to Florida. The reason for that was because of Claudia. I dated her for two and a half years before moving here. She was an epileptic and I cherished the ground she walked on. But, that threat with the gun was always in the back of my mind. That is why I never took advantage of her in any way."

"Aw, that's really nice," said Sandra, sloppily sentimental. "Claudia was your true lover." Suddenly she clouded. "I never had anybody to be nice to me. Well, Mom, I guess. She takes care of my little boy, but she tells me all the time how mixed up I am. I guess she's right. But with a life like mine, how could it be any other way?" She gulped down the last of her drink.

"Yeah, I know what you mean," he agreed.

That was enough conversation for Jerry. "Come on," he said to Sandra, putting his arm through hers to help steady her walk. "Let's go for a ride."

Before long, Stano was tired of her company. He was depressed and bored with her sad stories. He stopped the car along a deserted road and told her to get out. She was too drunk to realize the danger.

"I'm going to do you a favor," he told her. He struck her hard several times and took out his gun and shot her in the head. He left her body in a ditch and went home.

Eighteen

December 1979

Gerald Stano often visited Dale Mabry Boulevard, "The Strip," in Tampa on his long car rides. There he drove the several miles of motels and shops specializing in erotic sexual books and equipment. The street of gaudy neon signs started at the Mc-Dill Air Force Base gate and sprawled north past the Jai Alai, drive-in movies, and greasy spoon diners. In 1979, it extended past the airport and stadium to the northern edge of the city.

Dorothy Williams was a typical girl of this raunchy street. At age seventeen, she had a past that she was not proud to talk about. Although she was pretty and popular, she had dropped out of high school. Relations with her mother and stepfather were not good. They disapproved of many of her decisions, especially her working as a street prostitute in the town where they lived.

On December 10, 1979, a friend gave Dorothy a ride to a motel location where she often worked the street. Good lighting and ample room for cars to pull over enhanced her ability to see and be seen: see the john and strike a deal. If desired, the motel was cooperative and convenient.

Stano slowed down and eased the car over to the curb. "Want to party?" he inquired. She leaned in the window and quickly sized up the man and his car. *Clean wheels, mild-looking man, quick, easy score,* she decided.

"Sure," she said, "for the right price. What did you have in mind, baby?"

Jerry smiled. "Get in, honey. We'll burn a joint and talk about it."

"I'm Dot," she said, sliding into the front seat.

Jerry pulled away from the curb and entered the flow of traffic. As in every encounter with a female, Jerry soon provoked an argument and vented his rage. He severely beat her and stabbed her chest repeatedly.

In his confession several years later, he could not remember why he killed her.

Nineteen

In the early August 1982 meetings, Stano and Paul Crow both realized that their one-on-one cat and mouse game was over. Although both still enjoyed the game and had a mutual interest, it did not work as well anymore.

Stano's original six confessions were all in the Daytona Beach area or adjacent counties where Crow could call law enforcement people that he knew for help in identifying victims. During the last five confessions, law professionals from three Florida counties and two cities could not keep up with Stano's facts on victims because they covered seven years and almost one third of the state of Florida. Stano and Crow both knew that the investigation now had to be conducted

149

from a law enforcement level that could encompass all jurisdictions in order to identify the victims described by Stano.

Crow moved quickly. On August 25, 1982, a meeting was held in the Daytona Beach Office of Prosecutor Larry Nixon at Crow's request. The Florida Department of Law Enforcement (FDLE) conducted the meeting and many counties and cities were represented. They discussed the problem and decided to form a FDLE Task Force using local law officials to supplement the team. Plans were made to start operation of the Task Force quickly.

Stano was back in Florida State Prison awaiting further questioning. He was pleased with his renewed attention and publicity. The newspaper reported that a grand jury would be impaneled to hear new facts about Gerald Stano as a result of the last five confessions. The creation of the FDLE Task Force was also reported in the press.

In order to stay in the news, Stano was active from inside the prison. On August 27, he implicated Eddie Mann, who was in the Bradford County Jail, as his accomplice in the Bauer homicide. He and Eddie had known each other in high school.

Next, Stano made an independent move to expedite the confessions. He marked a Florida road map with over thirty murder victim locations with red dots and mailed it to the Jacksonville Florida F.B.I. Operations Center. There were many more dots on the map than there were confessions. His cellmate mailed the map for him on September 8, 1982. The same day, Stano was returned to the Daytona Beach jail for two weeks of questioning by the new FDLE Task Force.

The Tampa FDLE Operations Center and the Jacksonville FDLE Operations Center had compiled and coordinated the basic case information required to solve additional open homicides through questioning Stano. On September 9, Special Agent Ken Morrison and Paul Crow began a new, intense series of interviews with Jerry.

Meanwhile, the Jacksonville F.B.I. forwarded the Stano-marked victim location map to Crow in Daytona Beach. On September 11, Jerry agreed to elaborate on the map and to give firmer details to the Task Force. Jerry also discussed two open homicides on the Garden State Parkway in New Jersey and four homicides in Whitpain Township, Pennsylvania. During these interviews, Stano was questioned about thirty-five Florida West Coast murders. The Task Force tested him by including several previously solved murders. He admitted to only fifteen of these thirty-five and picked only from the unsolved cases. He passed the test and was obviously giving accurate information.

While the questioning sessions continued, other events were taking place. The FDLE Task Force requested the Brevard County Grand Jury to delay their investigation of Stano. The Task Force investigators needed additional time to question him about homicides throughout the state. The race to prosecute Stano in different counties made Jerry unavailable to the FDLE Task Force. On September 16, at a meeting in Orlando, a Tampa Task Force was formed under the direction of Special Agent Ed Williams to coordinate activities in Tampa.

On September 17, 1982, Stano confessed to the murders of Janine Ligotino and Ann Arceneaux in Gainesville, Florida in 1973. During a series of September taped interviews, he also confessed to the following murders:

Diana Lynn Valleck, Tampa, 1975
Bonnie Hughes, Polk County, 1976
Rose Oliver, Polk County, 1976
Enid Branch, Hillsborough County, 1976
Joan Gail Foster, Pasco County, 1977
Molly Newell, St. Petersburg, 1977

Phoebe Winston, Polk County, 1979
Emily Grieve, Pasco County, 1977
Christine Goodson, St. Petersburg, 1979
Madame X, Seminole County, 1974
Jane Doe, Hillsborough County, Unknown

On September 30, 1982, the Bradford County Grand Jury returned first-degree murder indictments on Eddie Mann and Gerald Stano for the murder of Barbara Bauer. Events were moving too quickly, and separate jurisdictions were starting to take independent actions ahead of the Task Force. There was a lack of coordination between cases. Also, all of those involved hungered for the press exposure that Stano's cases provided.

On October 1, 1982, Jerry Stano confessed to the murder of twelve-year-old Susan Basile in June 1975, at Port Orange, Florida. This confession was difficult to obtain because Stano did not want people to know that he had killed a child. Jerry also confessed to murdering thirteen-year-old Gail Joiner, but later retracted that confession. He was still not showing remorse, just concern about others' opinions of him. He knew, too, that child killers and rapists are despised and ostracized in prison.

On October 5, the Task Force began a series of field trips to substantiate the new confessions. At 8:45 A.M., a Hillsborough County Sheriff's Office aircraft picked up Jerry at the Daytona airport. The group included Paul Crow, Stano, FDLE Task Force and Hillsborough County Sheriff's Office representatives. Stano enjoyed the flight. Immediately after takeoff, he could identify DeLand on the right, and, as they crossed highway 17-92, Deltona, Sanford, and Orlando on the left. The route went directly over the south edge of Lake Apopka. The passengers identified the Florida Turnpike, Highway 27, and Disney World. Once past Disney, there was not much to see. Open country was to the north, and I-4 and Lakeland were to the south as they approached Plant City. The aircraft landed at the Plant City, Florida airport.

On the ground, the group traveled in a large motor home. The first stop was nearby Dover, Florida, where Jerry had left a hitchhiker between 1977 and 1979. Authorities had never received a report of a body in this location. The group visited four victim locations in Hillsborough County to the west. Later the same day, they drove back east to two victim locations in Polk County. They returned to Daytona Beach Airport at 9:30 that night.

The next morning the same procedure was repeated. The aircraft this day was from Pasco County, and their officers replaced Hillsborough on the inspection team with Crow, FDLE, and Stano. They flew to Pasco County Airport at Zepherhills, Florida, and landed. The morning was spent visiting five victims' burial sites in Pasco. After lunch, the group flew to St. Petersburg where six Pinellas County cases were reviewed and victim locations were examined. The night flight back was beautiful with lights identifying roads and cities. Although bad weather and turbulence made the last leg of the trip rough, Stano considered this high adventure. They arrived back at Daytona at 7:30 P.M.

Although not all confessions and site visits led to bodies, Stano did lead Florida officers to a total of nineteen locations where bodies had been found as he described. In other cases, he accurately described the missing victims and took officers to within a mile of where they were last seen. Urban growth had covered some locations with highways, malls, and parking lots. In remote areas, animals had likely scattered other remains.

The elapsed time since the murders, the changes in law enforcement personnel, and geographical changes made the West Coast cases much more difficult. Florida investigators were at a point where they needed to regroup and work in depth on specific cases. Some of the cases were close enough—with the evidence available and Stano's confession—to go to court.

Elsewhere, events involving Gerald Stano were rapidly moving forward. On October 7, 1982, he was charged with the first-degree murder of Barbara Bauer in Bradford County. The next day, he confessed to the November 1977 murder of Mary Kathleen Muldoon in Volusia County. This confession made a total of twenty-seven women whom he admitted killing in Florida from September 1973 to February 1980.

The recent series of FDLE flights, visits, and the growing number of police agencies involved made the Task Force unmanageable. On October 12, the Tampa media made public the expanding Gerald Stano investigation. Information leaks to the press by Task Force members complicated the investigation. Public pressure grew for more information on and the prosecution of the twenty new murder cases. Stano reveled in the publicity, notoriety, and attention. It was like a vacation from Florida State Prison travelling by air and mobile homes around Central Florida. He considered himself a national figure of historic significance.

During the last two weeks in October, he was visited by three Northern law enforcement representatives. Pennsylvania State Trooper William Davis interviewed Stano on several unsolved murders. Jerry denied involvement in those cases but did give details on four other stabbing murders during 1969 to 1972 in Whitpain Township where he had lived. He gave descriptions, told where he had met the victims, plus provided graphic details on how they were murdered and where their bodies were dumped.

Trooper Davis returned to Pennsylvania and reported this information, but results were fragmented. Local police searched the areas designated but found no bodies. At one location they found pieces of female undergarments and surmised from the evidence that a sexual encounter had been held there.

Locations near Willow Grove Naval Air Station provided no clues due to new construction.

The Philadelphia Inquirer and local Ambler and Springfield, Pennsylvania newspapers ran a series of articles in October and November 1982. These stories showed school photos of Stano, reported his early life, murder confessions, convictions to date in Florida, and presented him as a "mass murderer." The articles featured quotes from Doctor McMillan, Attorney Jacobson, and Officer Crow. The Pennsylvania cases were dropped in December 1982, due to lack of evidence.

The New Jersey interviews with Jerry involved the May 1969, Somers Point double slaying of college girls Susan David and Elizabeth Perry. The New Jersey officer in charge, Sgt. Robert Maholland, felt that the specifics of the confession did not match the circumstances of the crime. The details of the twelve-year-old murders closely matched the details of Stano's Florida beach area murders, however.

Although all investigators from Florida

and other states were advised of the interview techniques that were successful with Stano, some insisted on using standard interview practices. Jerry would lose interest without the challenge of the mental game, and thus valuable information would not be obtained. In addition, many law enforcement officers resent outside help in solving local cases, especially high visibility crimes like murder. So for various reasons, there were dissenting opinions on the validity of Stano's confessions in specific cases.

On October 29, 1982, Stano gave a deposition retracting his statements about Eddie Mann's involvement in the Bauer murder. An innocent man's nightmare was over. Eddie Mann was another of Stano's victims whose life continued but was permanently changed. Stano confided that eventually he was going to implicate Eddie or Roger, his brother. Police had considered possible participation in some crimes by others, but no evidence was ever found to substantiate this suspicion.

In a letter several years later, Stano explained this cruel joke he played upon Eddie Mann:

"I had stated first that Eddie was with me during this ordeal. Well, he wasn't at all. It was all fabricated about him. You see, we went to Junior High School together here in 1965. We were friends at one time, but his parents would treat me very nasty. They bought him everything he cried for, no matter the cost. That really rubbed me the wrong way from the start.

"I really felt nothing about Eddie getting arrested, 'cause I already had 75 years mandatory. Besides, I hated him, and wanted him to suffer like I did.

"But later, it started playing on my mind. Why should I involve someone else, when I was alone for the murder. I also said that I was staying at his parents' motel while I was down here then. That also was fabricated. It was just to get even with Eddie after those years."

On November 9, 1982, Stano was returned to Florida State Prison.

Twenty

March 21, 1973

The University of Florida is the core of life in Gainesville. Its sprawling campus has for years been the scene of young intellectuals' discussions and demonstrations which voice the mood of the times. In the early 1970s, the students were still clinging to the liberal hippie movement as reflected in their dress, guitar playing, and long hair. A slower Southern pace made the campus appear more like a Berkeley or Columbia of several years past.

Removed from college life altogether, yet desperately wanting to be part of events, were the misplaced young street people who hung around the fringes of the school. They were active in the sale of flowers on street corners, and they roamed through the night searching for any other opportunity to supplement their pitiful income. They were dropouts, runaways, and fugitives, but the experience of survival over time gave them a squatter's position resembling a gypsy camp. When others wandered into this subculture, they had to conform if they wanted to stay in peace.

Janine Marie Ligotino, nineteen, was one of the street people who believed that she was smart enough to survive. She had long dark hair and dark eyes. Her broad smile revealed chipped front teeth. She liked long skirts and sandals and hand-embroidered cotton shirts. Her friends would personalize inexpensive blouses with little flowers and other designs in exchange for her handmade paper flowers. She was originally from New York state and thought the mild Florida winters were great.

On the night of March 21, she was by herself when she met Ann Eugenia Arceneaux.

Ann's appearance was a lot like hers. Although of fair complexion with lighter long hair, her style was so similar that it suggested a sisterly connection. Ann's background, however, was completely different. She was an accelerated student who had graduated from high school a year early in

Silver Spring, Maryland. Now at seventeen, she was enjoying herself traveling around the country. She wore blue jeans and hiking boots and seemed confident that she could take care of herself.

At midnight everything on the block near the edge of town was closed. The two girls huddled under a florist awning in the heavy rain.

A green Plymouth Satellite blinked its lights and pulled over. The driver, Gerald Stano, smiled, rolled down the window, and asked directions. When the girls assured him that they could show him the way, he patted the seat and they got in. He had already had a lot to drink and was now having another beer. He didn't particularly like these two damp figures getting into the front seat of his new car, but he thought they looked pretty good. He offered them a beer, but they were finishing a large bottle of Coke that they passed between them. Soon he bluntly said that he would like to have sex with both of them. Janine, who was sitting in the middle, looked at her friend, and they both laughed out loud.

"Guess we'll have that beer after all." They drove silently along some back roads and finally he asked them for sex again.

"We don't think so. Not with a pig like you," Ann replied, feeling fairly secure since there were two of them.

His expression and eyes were so cold when he looked at them that they were scared into silence. Only the windshield wipers made a sound.

Then Janine, sitting next to him, started to tease him. "Oh come on, lighten up! It's not you especially. We're different, you know, close friends." She put a hand on his leg. "Ann gets upset with me when I flirt with men," she giggled.

"Cut that out," Ann bristled.

Stano reached down under the seat. Jan yelled, "My God, no!" Jerry sat back up with a large hunting knife in hand. He slapped Ann hard. Janine started screaming. He lunged across Janine to stab Ann under the arm. Janine held up her hand to protect her face, and he cut her right hand and made a deep slash on her left knee.

Jerry continued yelling, slashing at both of them. Ann struggled to unlock the door. The lock releases were cylindrical and designed to deter theft — and escape. He stopped the car near the dark intersection of North East Tenth Avenue and Eighteenth Street. An old, white wooden church stood nearby. With his victims bleeding and hyster-

164

ical, he strangled Janine until she was motionless. Then he ran around and opened the door to let the bleeding Ann make a run for her life. He liked a chase before the kill.

She managed to walk and crawl about two hundred feet before she collapsed. Stano straddled the woman, grasped the hunting knife with both hands and plunged it deep between her breasts.

Panting, he looked over toward his car and realized that Janine was now awake and had witnessed the slaughter. *No need to hurry,* he thought, as he walked deliberately back toward the car. *The bitch is pretty badly cut up, and probably can't move at all.* The car door hung open. He gazed for a moment at the small whimpering figure in her blood soaked embroidered blouse. As she pleaded for her life, she realized that there was no escape from this maniac.

Stano dragged her from his car into the thicket about fifty feet from Ann's body. There he stabbed her to death, thirteen times in all.

Stano spent a long time cleaning his car because the two murders had been especially messy. He did a very thorough job of disposing of any evidence.

Police spent thousands of hours searching for clues in the murder of Ann Arceneaux and Janine Ligotino. No one could have imagined that a psychopath had driven over a thousand miles, murdered the two girls, and then returned to Pennsylvania, all in three days' time.

Crow said that he was getting very tired of talking to Jerry. They joked back and forth before Crow admitted his frustration with the lengthy talks, and he asked how much more time it would take.

Stano replied, "Well, we are ninety-eight percent done."

Crow stroked his mustache and asked as calmly as possible, "Then how about cluing me in on the other two percent?"

"Well, I killed two girls in Gainesville," Stano remarked casually.

"Why didn't you tell me in 1980 that you killed two up in Gainesville?" Crow asked, his voice rising.

"Dumb luck," was Stano's answer.

Crow was sitting directly across the desk and as he picked up the phone he asked what year the Gainesville murders occurred.

166

"It was 1976, or something like that," Stano mumbled.

Crow knew that Jerry was always screwed up with the years, that he had a problem with numbers. Yet, he was so exact in describing clothing and jewelry, and so detailed in exactly how he committed the murders.

Crow completed the call to Gainesville and asked if they had a murder up there in 1976 with two girls involved. The answer was a flat no. When Crow told them that he had a guy sitting right there telling him all about it, the officer on the other end of the line showed interest but said he'd have to check further. He called back a short time later.

"Well, it wasn't in '76, but we had one in '73 with two girls killed at the same time."

Crow covered the phone to ask, "You didn't kill two at the same time, did you?"

"Yeah," Stano answered. "One had boots on. I could chase her down outside the car. The other one had gypsy clothes on." He was obviously turned on recounting the tale. "She had a tall Coke bottle with her and she sat in the middle. The other girl with boots on wore slacks and a blouse."

"How can you remember all of this?" Crow asked. "You are a sick son of a bitch, you know that?"

167

Stano smiled, delighted with this reaction. "I pulled a knife out and started stabbing the one in the middle, and the one on the right couldn't get the locks up fast enough. She finally got them up and ran, but I was able to catch her because she wore those boots."

Crow later recalled that when he got the crime scene photographs one of the victims was lying there with boots on, the other one had gypsy clothing.

Later, Sergeant Jesse Blitch of the Gainesville Police Department met with Stano in Crow's office and taped Stano's confession to these murders.

Gerald Eugene Stano, as he looked when he attended Seabreeze Junior High School in Daytona Beach.

Stano in Wissahickon High School, 1971.

Police shot of Stano upon his 1981 arrest.

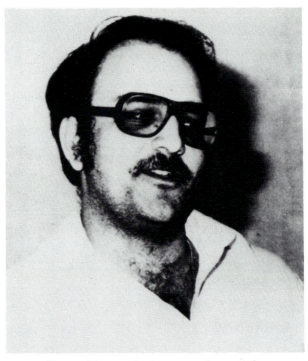

Stano after nearly two years in custody.
(*AP/Wide World*)

TWENTY-TWO IDENTIFIED VICTIMS
OF GERALD EUGENE STANO

Ann Arceneaux, 17

Janine Marie Ligotino, 19

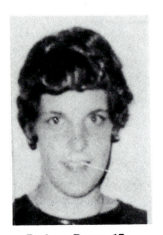

Barbara Bauer, 17

Cathy Lee Scharf, 17

Nancy Heard, 24

Diana Lynn Valleck, 18

Susan Basile, 12

Linda Ann Hamilton, 16

 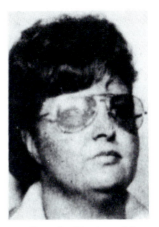

Susan Bickrest, 24   Bonnie Hughes, 34

Ramona Neal, 18

Emily Branch, 21

Joan Gail Foster, 18

Molly Newell, 20

Emily Grieve, 38

Phoebe Winston, 23

Mary Kathleen Muldoon, 23   **Sandra DuBose, 34**

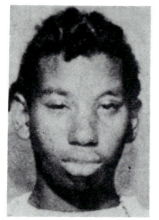

Christine Goodson, 17

Dorothy Williams, 17

Mary Carol Maher, 20

Toni Van Haddocks, 26

RED DOTS INDICATE LOCATIONS
OF STANO'S MURDER VICTIMS

Stano marked a Florida road map with red dots, indicating the locations where he'd dumped thirty of his victims, and sent it to the F.B.I. Operations Center in Jacksonville.

The decomposed upper torso of Cathy Lee Scharf was found on January 19, 1974 by hunters just north of Titusville, Florida.

Nancy Heard, as she was found by police.

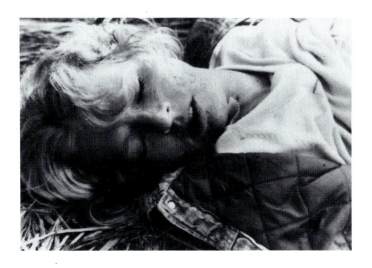

Linda Hamilton's nude, brutally beaten body was found by fishermen on July 22, 1975 at Turtle Mound, east of the Indian River.

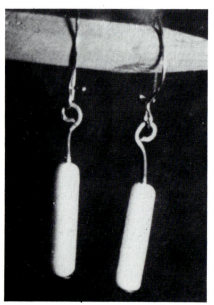

Linda Hamilton wore only these pierced earrings when her body was found.

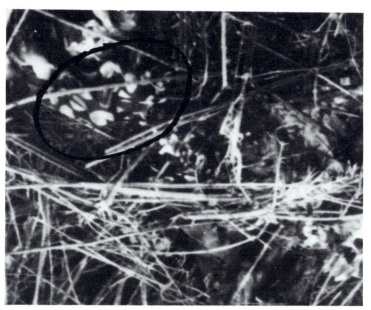

The skeletal remains of Ramona Neal were found on June 15, 1976 by a motorcyclist along the Old Dixie Highway. A blue polka dot bikini was found over the skeleton.

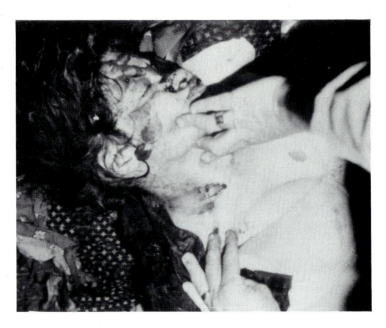

Partially blind when murdered, Sandra DuBose as she was
found on August 5, 1978 in a Brevard County roadside ditch.

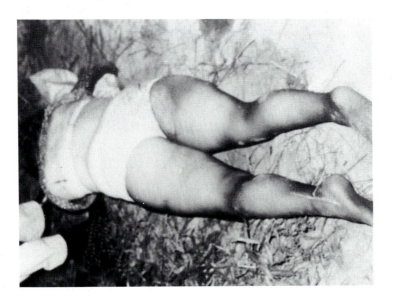

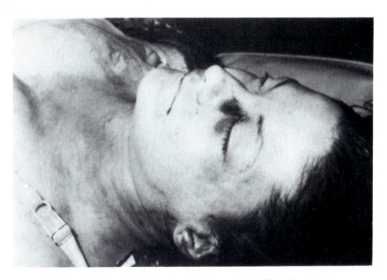

Sandra DuBose's body, just before the official autopsy.

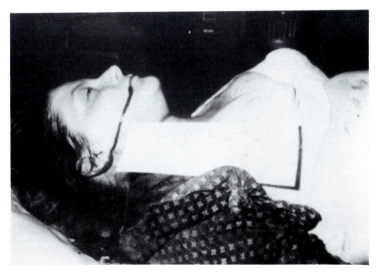

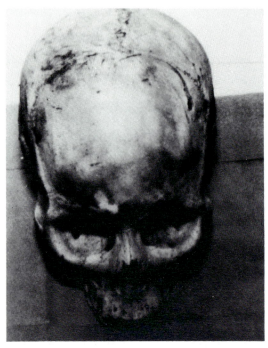

The skull of Toni Van Haddocks was found along with her partial skeleton.

Stano's immaculately maintained green Plymouth Duster in which he killed many of his victims.

Police detective Paul Crow at his desk at the time of his investigation into the Stano murders.

Paul Crow interviewing Stano.

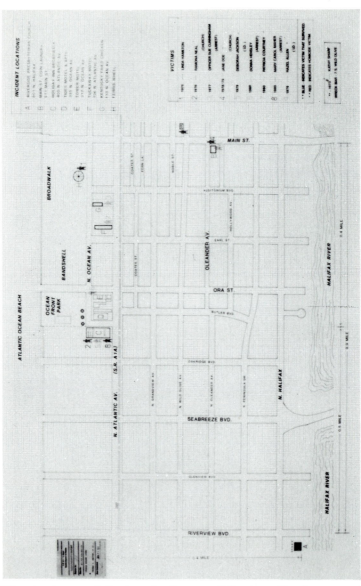

The street map of the boardwalk area of Daytona Beach, prepared by Paul Crow to aid his testimony in Federal District Court.

Lawrence J. Nixon, Chief Assistant State Attorney, Seventh Judicial Circuit Court was the prosecutor in the two Volusia County Stano trials.

Judge S. James Foxman, Seventh Judicial Court, pronounces the death sentence on Stano for the murders of Susan Bickrest and Kathleen Muldoon.

Stano grimaces as he is sentenced to death. He is flanked by his attorney, Howard Pearl, and Belle Turner, State Attorney's Office.

Twenty-one

November 11, 1977

That night, Jerry Stano drove down Seabreeze Boulevard and stopped at the Silver
Bucket. After selecting a table and ordering
drinks, he couldn't keep his eyes off his
waitress. But everytime he tried to talk to
her, she was polite but cool. Rejection was
the last thing he needed. He picked up his
drink and moved over toward an empty bar
stool. He passed close by her and liked the
smell of her perfume.

"How about going out after work?" he
whispered. "I can show you some fun."

"I'm sorry, I have a date," she said flatly
and walked on.

"Try another station," chuckled the man
on the bar stool next to him. "That one's
got a lot of interference."

What a bitch, he thought and finished his drink. *So much for Mister Nice Guy.* He walked out to the parking lot and waited for closing time.

Finally she came out alone. She was very attractive. Her brown hair was long on the shoulders of her corduroy pantsuit. She took long strides across the parking lot coming unknowingly close to Stano's car. As she approached, he leaned over and pushed open the door on the passenger's side.

Startled for a moment, she recognized the man. "Look, guy," she smiled, "I told you earlier. I'm not interested."

He brought the gun up from the seat and pointed the .22 automatic directly at her. "Get in," he ordered quietly. She did.

"Put that gun away," she managed to say as they drove off. "There's no need for that."

"That's better," he smiled and stuck the gun in the waistband of his pants.

"Want to stop for a drink," she suggested.

"You know what I want," he sneered and pushed his heavy glasses back on his nose.

They were at the beach now and the waves were crashing in. He clasped her throat and tried to kiss her, but she pushed him back. He ripped her blouse and tore at her pants.

"I don't want to have sex with you," she screamed. She felt for his gun. He intercepted and forced her hand to rub his crotch. She made a fist and tried to pound him. He jerked her fist up to her own chin and slammed his elbow hard across her breast. He slapped her in the face with the back of his hand, and this time he knocked her out.

He started the car, crossed the river to U.S. 1, and headed south toward New Smyrna Beach. When he came to a dark, desolate spot, he pulled over to the side of the road. She stirred.

"Get out of the car," he ordered. He pushed her and slid across the seat beside her.

"Alright," she sobbed. "Just don't kill me."

He slapped her down and pieces of shell became embedded in her knees. He unzipped his pants and pressed her head against his penis, demanding a blow job. While she was sobbing and choking, Jerry grinned, and pressed the gun to the right side of her head. He pulled the trigger while his penis was still in her mouth.

Death was not instantaneous, however, even though the bullet entered her brain. He pushed her into a drainage ditch by the side of the road. Tidal action from nearby Turnbull Bay filled the ditch with water. Finally, the girl drowned.

The next day, a woman discovered the body in nine inches of water. Her body was fully clothed but she wore no underpants or shoes. The time and the water had removed all proof of sexual activity, but her body still gave graphic evidence of the previous night of total horror.

The young waitress was identified as Mary Kathleen Muldoon, 23, known as Katie. She was an orphan and part-time working student at Daytona Beach Community College.

The murder remained unsolved until Stano's 1982 confession. He accurately described the victim's clothes and led police to the exact spot in the ditch where her body was found.

Twenty-two

Stano's new confessions to the Florida Department of Law Enforcement Task Force started a media storm. Headlines called him a "mass murderer" and a nonchalant killer of thirty-nine women. Articles compared him to David Berkowitz, "Son of Sam" killer of five; Albert DeSalvo, "Boston Strangler" killer of eighteen; John Wayne Gacy, killer of thirty-three; Patrick Kearney, killer of twenty-one; and Ted Bundy, convicted killer of three and suspect in twenty other murders. Stano, if his confessions were true, had killed more people than any American in the Twentieth Century.

As Jerry sat in Florida State Prison, he felt pleased with himself. Ironically, the new kind of attention he received inside the prison was not what he wanted or expected. When he was assigned his new cell, Stano experienced a series of threatening incidents.

He got a letter from Carol Bundy, Ted's wife. Although her letter was very polite, she asked Stano if he ". . . had any knowledge of the homicides of which Ted was convicted?" Jerry felt threatened by this letter. Ted Bundy was on Death Row at Florida State Prison and was respected by the inmates. Stano imagined all sorts of ways that runners or agents of Bundy could pressure him, even harm him, to force his cooperation.

Stano wrote to Don Jacobson, his former lawyer, and requested that he contact Ed Williams and Tim Elder of FDLE Task Force to tell them of his fears. These men had Stano placed in Q-Wing for safety purposes, but he did not feel safe.

In an unrelated incident, Donald Perry, the cell occupant next to Stano, started calling Stano "his baby." He demanded part of Jerry's canteen order, ". . . so nobody will hurt you." He told Jerry, "Nobody can have you but me." Other inmates demanded money and told Stano that they were going to make him a "boy" or prostitute if he

174

didn't pay up.

Then, six newspaper articles were placed in Stano's bars one night with a note that said, "You are a dead man, Stano."

These incidents were also relayed by letter to the lawyer, Jacobson. He responded to Mrs. Bundy and forwarded her request to Paul Crow. Jacobson also forwarded Jerry's concerns about his welfare to the police. Finally, Jacobson wrote Jerry a letter that he could show to others saying that Jerry had been declared a pauper and was in no position to do financial favors.

Jerry's family visited him about every two weeks at Florida State Prison. After the FDLE confessions, the only way the Stano family could rationalize Jerry's actions was to revive their hopes of having him declared insane and committed. Jerry found this argument appealing because it would keep him out of the electric chair, and might possibly lead to his release in the future.

In January 1983, Jerry was taken to Hillsborough County on the Gail Joiner case. He took investigators to within a mile of where the girl was last seen.

But, Hillsborough County Sheriff's personnel had trouble dealing with Stano and his "mental games." They gave him a PSE examination in addition to Sodium Pentothal. They reported that he passed one and failed the other. Gail Joiner's body was not found, and Stano was returned to Florida State Prison. Stano still enjoyed the cat and mouse game, but only if the other players knew how to play.

On January 11, 1983, Stano was taken to Dade City Court House to give depositions in cases in Pinellas and Pasco Counties.

On January 18, while he was still in Hillsborough County, the Grand Jury of Volusia County indicted him for first-degree murder for the murders of Susan Bickrest and Katie Muldoon.

He tried to call attorney Don Jacobson, but could not reach him. After Jerry returned to Florida State Prison, he wrote Jacobson a letter in February where he stated that if he could not get a not guilty by reason of insanity ruling, then he would ask the court for the death sentence. He said that he and his parents were prepared for it. He asked Jacobson to "get with" assistant public defender Howard Pearl and Judge Foxman. Jerry related this intention several times in letters made public by his subsequent attorneys. He either wanted to be out of prison or in prison with status and class. Considering this value judgment of Jerry's, his subsequent conduct in plea hearings and sentencing is logical.

On March 3, 1983, Stano was indicted for the murder of Cathy Scharf in Brevard County. The following week he was moved from Florida State Prison to the jail at Starke, Florida, just fifteen minutes south, on Monday, March 7. There with his newly court-appointed counsel, Fredrick Replogle, he appeared before Judge John J. Crews in the Circuit Court for Bradford County. Also present were Thomas M. Ewell, an Assistant State Attorney in Bradford County and Kenneth C. Herbert, an Assistant State Attorney in Alachua County.

Three cases were before the court. Two of the cases had been transferred from Alachua County and involved the murders of Ann Arceneaux and Janine Ligotino. These were consolidated with the Bradford County Barbara Bauer case.

Herbert tendered Stano's guilty plea for

177

the two Alachua County cases, and Replogle formally changed the Stano plea in the Bauer case from not guilty to guilty. Judge Crews appointed the Public Defender Replogle to represent Stano in the Arceneaux and Ligotino Alachua County cases.

Alachua County had an agreement with Stano that he would receive concurrent sentences on the two cases. This agreement did not affect the Bauer case.

Stano was sworn by the court. Judge Crews made sure that he understood all nineteen paragraphs of his petition to change his plea from not guilty to guilty. The Judge then explained the Alachua County plea bargain for concurrent sentences and that it did not affect the Bradford County case. Finally, Stano was advised that a plea of guilty in these three cases could be used as an aggravating circumstance in other cases if the state should seek a death penalty. He was reminded that the life sentence included a mandatory twenty-five-year minimum term. Stano indicated that he understood all of the points and was satisfied with his representation.

Stano's three guilty pleas were accepted

on the three counts of murder. Next, the factual basis of the three cases were established by the two prosecutors.

Judge Crews found Gerald Stano guilty of murder on each count and sentenced him to three terms of life imprisonment.

Gerald Stano now had admitted the murder of nine women in court and had been charged in six murders and received six life sentences with seventy-five years minimum to serve.

In March of 1983, Stano was taken to the Court House in Daytona Beach to plead in the Volusia County murder cases of Bickrest and Muldoon. At Stano's request, he went before Judge Foxman in his chambers.

Jerry eased himself into one of the comfortable green leather chairs around the large conference table in Judge Foxman's chambers. He smiled at the thought of sitting side by side with lawyers and a judge. Their importance made him feel more significant. Law books lined the walls and muffled out courthouse noise in this inner sanctuary. The court reporter entered and eyed Stano nervously as she set up her machine. Her trim figure caught Jerry's eye, and he tried unsuccessfully to engage her in small talk. He didn't see many women in prison. After everyone was in place around the oak table, Judge Foxman appeared and briskly took his seat at the head of the table. Hearings are often conducted in chambers where the judge can shed his robes.

Stano was accompanied by his new court-appointed attorney, Howard Pearl. Larry Nixon represented the State. All of the men knew each other from previous Stano cases.

During the sentencing for the Maher, Van Haddocks and Heard murders, Judge Foxman had told Stano that his acts deserved punishment by death, but the court deal precluded the death sentence. There was no such deal for the Bickrest and Muldoon murders.

Judge Foxman opened the proceedings by identifying the two cases and acknowledging the people present.

Howard Pearl advised the judge that Stano was ready for arraignment and that he intended to plead guilty to each of the first-degree murder charges. He stated that Stano also wished to waive the sentencing jury and have the judge determine sentence in the two cases.

Pearl also stated that Stano had not received from the State all of the facts concerning the two cases. The delay was caused because the State did not yet have all of the materials in each of Stano's prior cases, since three murder cases had just been completed four days earlier in another county. The state and defense had agreed that the materials in all the cases should be collected and delivered at once rather than incrementally. Therefore, Pearl was not fully prepared to advise Stano whether or not the State had sufficient evidence to convict him. Pearl wanted all present to know that Stano knew that Pearl could not advise him whether to seek a trial by jury. But, despite his attorney's advice to continue the case, Stano was adamant about pleading guilty right away.

He had advised his lawyer that his confessions were made voluntarily, competently, and intelligently after proper warning of his rights. There was no apparent legal reason why the confessions would be suppressed. Stano had advised his lawyer that he wanted to enter his plea now rather than go through a trial or delay because he was guilty.

When the defense attorney finished,

Judge Foxman asked Stano if he had any comments on his lawyer's statements. Stano said that he had no additional comments and agreed that it was his decision to proceed to enter a guilty plea without further delay.

Nixon explained that the evidence to prove beyond a reasonable doubt that Stano committed each of the homicides had been provided to the defense during the discovery phase of the case. The evidence not yet available concerned other cases and were relevant only during the sentencing phase of the case rather than proof of the Bickrest and Muldoon murders.

Gerald Stano was sworn, and began his testimony. The judge referred to the extensive psychiatric evaluations, and the judge and Stano agreed that he was competent to stand trial. Judge Foxman then went into a long and detailed discussion of the normal murder jury trial procedure and, if guilty, the jury sentence recommendation phase. He also explained the two possible Florida sentences in first-degree murder cases: life with a twenty-five-year mandatory minimum and death.

The judge explained to Stano that by taking the jury out of the proceedings he was leaving the sentence to the sole decision of the judge. Stano stated that he understood what he was doing, had discussed it with his lawyer, and had no questions.

Stano was arraigned for the murders of Mary Kathleen Muldoon and Susan Bickrest and entered guilty pleas for both. After the pleas, the judge made sure that Stano understood the meaning of the guilty pleas, that they were voluntary, and then he listed all the trial and appeal rights that Stano was waiving. The judge reaffirmed that Stano was satisfied with his attorney and had no questions for him or the court.

Stano was doing exactly what he thought was rational. He was pleading guilty to murders that he had committed and was seeking swift judgment. He wanted the freedom of being judged insane or the prestige and benefits of living on Death Row at Florida State Prison. In Stano's opinion, he could not lose.

Judge Foxman and Howard Pearl were cautious. Each was trying to do his appointed job; Pearl serving the accused, Foxman serving the law. Neither understood Stano's behavior. Both knew Stano was far too smart not to know what he was doing, but neither man could understand his sense of urgency.

Prosecutor Nixon presented the State's evidence to support the factual basis for the charges and pleas. Upon his motion, the supporting documents of the two cases were entered, such as death certificates, confessions, investigation reports, and photos. Defense Attorney Pearl made sure that they were admitted for plea only, not for sentencing.

Larry Nixon completed the presentation of evidence for each case, and Judge Foxman ruled it sufficient to support the guilty pleas. In both cases Gerald Stano entered formal guilty pleas, which were accepted by the court. Stano was found guilty of two counts of first-degree murder, with no deal to protect him from death. The sentencing phase would be in two months, on May 18, 1983.

Twenty-three

Gerald Stano was back in administrative custody in Florida State Prison and back in the news as well after his conviction in five murder one cases in three counties in one week. The prison population was involved in discussing every aspect of the Stano news, but they remained puzzled by two factors.

First, why did Stano confess to all of those murders when he was not a suspect and the authorities had no evidence? Second, why did he continue to receive life and a minimum twenty-five years in the Alachua and Bradford County murders with no plea bargain to avoid the death penalty? These issues generated a lot of discussion among the inmates.

His fellow prisoners did not trust Stano's motives. First of all, no one inside prison trusts law enforcement officials, but Stano trusted Paul Crow. Second, inmates assume that all other prisoners want to be out in society rather than more comfortable in prison. Yet, all Stano wanted was R Wing privileges.

But what Stano was trying to achieve was simple: either a verdict of not guilty by reason of insanity or guilty and death. His in-between status bothered him a great deal. He looked forward to May 18 when Judge Foxman was due to sentence him on the Bickrest and Muldoon murders.

His attorney, Howard Pearl, requested and received a delay until June 8, 1983 for the Bickrest and Muldoon sentencing hearings. On that day in the Daytona Beach Courthouse the proceeding began.

Judge S. James Foxman presided in his usual precise manner. He methodically identified the two cases, instructed the recorder to indicate that the proceeding was in open court, and identified as present Stano, Pearl, and Larry Nixon for the State. He outlined the plea hearing in March where Stano entered two guilty pleas and elected to waive a jury for sentencing. The judge

186

summarized that Stano had been found guilty by the court and today's proceeding was for sentence hearings in both cases. Next, Judge Foxman reminded all present that two cases were being sentenced. He cautioned that some information was appropriate in both cases and some testimony would apply specifically to one case or the other. Finally, a schedule of witnesses and the presentation of factual circumstances surrounding the two homicides was discussed and agreed upon by the court, state, and defense. Witnesses would be called during the morning. Psychiatric interviews would be held in the afternoon and early next morning, and then court would reconvene for the balance of the witnesses.

Before proceeding with the case, Larry Nixon and Howard Pearl agreed that an inquiry should be made of the accused to insure that he was not uncomfortable with Judge Foxman hearing his cases. Judge Foxman, in the Maher, Van Haddocks, and Heard sentencing, had used strong language indicating that Stano deserved the death penalty. Now he would be sentencing two cases with no prior agreement in place. Death penalty cases always have extensive appellate review, and this inquiry was requested as a caution against future review.

Judge Foxman agreed that the inquiry should be made and asked that Stano be put under oath, and he asked that Howard Pearl conduct the inquiry since it concerned the judge. Stano was sworn and examined, then testified.

Stano acknowledged the earlier cases where Judge Foxman presided and affirmed that he had no objection to him. He agreed that the judge would be fair and not be prejudiced. Stano reaffirmed his guilty pleas and his desire to proceed without a sentencing jury.

The judge made a general inquiry to insure that Stano was satisfied with his attorney and had no complaints or questions about the proceedings.

"This is the way you want to do it, then?" he was finally asked.

"Yes, sir!" he replied crisply.

Pearl then asked the court to consider his motion to suppress the testimony of Probation and Parole Officer Edward C. Seltzer, and to suppress the use of his Presentence Investigation (PSI) Report. Pearl argued that the interviews were conducted without any Miranda warnings, that defense counsel was not notified in advance of the interviews and, most importantly, that original information was in the report that could not be established otherwise. This information was highly incriminating and provided aggravating circumstances.

Nixon noted that the State had announced its intention not to call Parole Officer Seltzer for testimony. The State agreed with the interpretation that the PSI report could not be used as a source of fact to sustain a statutory aggravating circumstance.

Judge Foxman ruled that Seltzer's testimony or PSI report would not be used to establish aggravating factors for the purpose of a sentence hearing. Both counsel agreed that the report could be made part of the court file.

All witnesses present were then sworn by the clerk. They were asked to remain outside the courtroom, instructed not to discuss the case with anyone except either attorney, and told that they would be called as soon as possible. After all witnesses left the courtroom, the bailiff reported, "They're out of hearing."

The judge thanked the bailiff and asked counsel for brief opening statements. Nixon was first and stated that pursuant to section 921, Florida statutes, evidence would be presented to sustain four aggravating circumstances in support of the death penalty for the murders of Katie Muldoon and Susan Bickrest. The state is limited to presenting evidence which is directed to the aggravating factors listed in the statutes. The four subsections which Nixon sought to establish were: first, that the defendant was previously convicted of another capital felony; second, that the capital felony was committed while the defendant was engaged in the commission of or attempt to commit a number of enumerated felonies; third, that the capital felony was especially heinous, atrocious, and cruel; fourth, that the capital felony and homicides were committed in a cold, calculated, and premeditated manner without any pretense of moral or legal justification.

Pearl proposed that the defendant would establish two statutory mitigating circumstances which would outweigh the aggravating circumstances presented by the State.

The two statutory mitigating circumstances Pearl sought to establish concerned mental status, and were: first, that the capital felony was committed while the defendant was under the influence of extreme mental or emotional disturbance; and second, that the capacity of the defendant to appreciate the criminality of his conduct or to conform his conduct to the requirements of law was substantially impaired. In addition, three nonstatutory mitigating circumstances would be presented. These would include defendant's early history and disastrous marriage. Also included would be the confessions and guilty pleas saving the State time and money and clearing of uncertainties for victims' families.

Dr. Arthur Schwartz was the first witness called by the State. He was stipulated to be qualified as an expert in forensic pathology. Six pictures were introduced and marked as evidence. Four pertained to Susan Bickrest's autopsy and two pertained to the autopsy of Muldoon. Testimony on Bickrest was first.

The doctor testified that Susan Bickrest had a swollen and bruised left eye which occurred before death. Her lower teeth had cut the inside of her lower lip from a blow. He stated that she had been manually strangled with two hands. This established that

Susan had suffered before death, rendering her murder heinous, atrocious, or cruel. There was also evidence of drowning in a shallow place. Her death could not have been a suicide or accident. The doctor's testimony established that the cause of death was manual strangulation and drowning.

Next, Dr. Schwartz was questioned about the autopsy he performed on Mary Kathleen Muldoon. He testified that her body was examined at the Halifax Medical Center Morgue. She had a penetrating gunshot wound into the right temple. The bullet went approximately three quarters of the way through the brain. The gun was fired at close contact because the wound entrance was stained with a ring of gunpowder. This evidence established that the murder was conducted in a cold and calculated manner, like an execution.

Muldoon's lungs were voluminous, overinflated, and there was evidence of pulmonary edema in the airways indicating drowning. The cause of death was entered as a gunshot wound to the head and drowning.

Five pictures of Muldoon were offered as evidence. Four were accepted and entered as evidence. From the pictures, the doctor testified that deposits of sand and coquina shells on her knees indicated that Muldoon was possibly kneeling when shot. Another photograph showed the powder ring around the bullet entry which indicated that the gun was fired at close range.

Dr. Schwartz testified that the bullet did not give direct or indirect injury to the brain stem and therefore death was definitely not instantaneous. Death came within an hour due to drowning. This evidence established that Muldoon also suffered before dying. After his testimony, Dr. Schwartz was excused.

Dr. Arthur Botting, current District Medical Examiner, was called as the next State witness. His expert qualifications were stipulated by counsel and were accepted by the judge and he was sworn as a witness. Pearl had Dr. Botting examine the autopsy protocol and medical examiner's file in both the Bickrest and Muldoon cases. In both cases, Dr. Botting did not feel that the data confirmed a finding of death by drowning. He confirmed that Bickrest was manually strangled and that Muldoon was shot in the head at close range. He could not support the drowning findings from the data available. Dr. Botting readily acknowledged that he had not participated in the actual autopsy in either case, and his opinions were qualified by that factor.

Pearl stipulated with Nixon that Detective Lewis, the next witness, was an expert in the fingerprint field. When an accused is convicted of murder, his fingerprints are put on the court record of the judgment of guilt. Lewis identified Gerald Stano's fingerprints on six prior murder convictions as proof of the aggravating circumstances of conviction of a prior violent felony.

Judge Foxman announced that the psychiatrists' reexaminations would take place in the jury room. The judge also asked both counsel to be available during the afternoon in case of any questions. It was agreed that the two Gainesville psychiatrists would testify first tomorrow, following their examinations. They would be followed by the local psychiatrists and then the police officers.

Court was recessed for lunch. The two doctors' examinations were held in the afternoon, two more in the morning of June 9, 1983, and court was reconvened at 10:20 A.M.

* * *

Court was called to order by the bailiff. Judge Foxman instructed that the same rules for spectators were in effect, once court opened that no one could leave until a break. Then he said, "Gentlemen, let's continue the hearing at this time. I believe you have reached a stipulation."

Pearl outlined that to the court. Dr. McMillan was living in Wyoming and could not arrive for several days. Nixon and Pearl agreed that if asked two questions she would answer that in her opinion, within reasonable medical probability, when Gerald Stano committed both murders, he was under the influence of extreme mental or emotional disturbance. Further, in her opinion, the capacity of the defendant to appreciate the criminality of his conduct or to conform his conduct to the requirements of law was substantially impaired. Pearl proffered her testimony to establish the two statutory mental mitigating factors.

After a brief discussion, Judge Foxman accepted this. Then Drs. Barnard, Carrera, and Stern were called and sworn. The rule requiring witnesses not to hear other witnesses' testimony was waived by the defendant for the three psychiatrists. Pearl and Nixon explained to the court that a set of copies of all written psychiatric reports would be presented for each of the two cases as evidence together at a later time. The court agreed.

The doctors were expected to answer the two basic questions involving the statutory mitigating circumstances that Dr. McMillan answered. Each were called by the State and the Defense.

Dr. Frank Carrera, Gainesville, Florida, was called first. When questioned by Mr. Nixon, he testified that as to both murders: "Stano was not under the influence of extreme mental or emotional disturbance. His capacity to conform his conduct was not substantially impaired."

Howard Pearl cross-examined Dr. Carrera intently on emotional disturbance and specifically anger, trying to modify his answers. The doctor would not waver and summarized: "In neither case under question today was Mr. Stano, from his own description or from other information, totally out of conscious control of his behavior; that, from my understanding of the events presented to me, Mr. Stano never lost total control of his thinking, of his actions and of planful behavior."

Dr. George W. Barnard, Gainesville, Florida, was called. When questioned by Mr. Nixon, he testified for both murders that: "Stano was not under the influence of extreme mental or emotional disturbance. His capacities to appreciate and conform his conduct were not substantially impaired."

When cross-examined by Pearl, Dr. Barnard acknowledged that Stano had some impairment. He said, ". . . I think the impairment was that, basically, he was in a situation wherein he did not really take into consideration the other person as a person and, in that sense, tended to dehumanize the situation."

Dr. Barnard would not agree that this was a "substantial" impairment as required by the statute. After both counsel finished their examinations, the doctors were excused.

Dr. Fernando Stern, Daytona Beach, was called and examined by Pearl. He stated, "It is my expert clinical opinion that Mr. Stano was under the influence of mental and emotional disturbance in both cases. In my opinion, the capacity of the defendant to appreciate the criminality of his conduct was unimpaired. He knew that it was criminal. I believe that he was not able to conform his conduct to the requirements of the law, that this was substantially impaired."

Nixon did not cross-examine, and Dr. Stern was excused. Dr. Robert Davis, Daytona Beach, was called next, duly sworn and examined. When questioned by Nixon about Stano being under the influence of extreme mental or emotional disturbance, Dr. Davis replied: "In my opinion, Mr. Stano is a sociopathic personality, antisocial personality. And this is considered a mental illness." He could not offer an opinion as to the influence of mental or emotional disturbance on his actions.

When questioned about Stano's capacity to appreciate the criminality of his conduct or the capacity to conform his conduct to the requirements of law being substantially impaired, he answered: "Under those circumstances, I feel that he appreciated the extent and nature of his acts." He added that he did not believe there was any substantial impairment.

In his cross-examination, Pearl tried to have Dr. Davis relate Stano's marital problems to his anger and subsequent behavior.

Dr. Davis found little correlation and no relation of this marital-related anger to his victims in these murders.

After the lunch break, the State called the next witness. Nixon asked the bailiff to bring in Don Goodson. He identified himself as Donald Joseph Goodson, Acting Chief of Police of New Smyrna Beach. Under examination, he reported the facts surrounding the reporting and recovery of Mary Kathleen Muldoon's corpse in November 1977. The scene was a remote wooded area off Turnbull Street in the north end of New Smyrna Beach. The body was found lying facedown in approximately nine to ten inches of water in a drainage ditch. Three pictures of the exact area were entered into evidence. The questions and his testimony then switched to Stano.

Chief Goodson reported that about October 9, 1982, he and Sgt. Paul Crow of Daytona Beach, interviewed Stano as a suspect in the Muldoon murder. Then later on November 12, 1982, with Sgt. Paul Crow and Agent Tim Elder of the Florida Department of Law Enforcement, Stano sat in the right front seat of a vehicle and they proceeded south on U.S. 1 into New Smyrna Beach. Mr. Stano had stated previously that he could possibly take the officers to the scene where Miss Muldoon's body had been found. Following Stano's directions, the car went into New Smyrna Beach and turned around and went back north on U.S. 1. As they passed the city limit, they turned around again and proceeded south. As they passed Turnbull Street for the third time, Stano made a reference that it was possibly the street. At his direction the car turned around and entered the dirt road where the body had been found. All got out of the vehicle and Stano walked about two hundred yards, stopped, looked around, and identified the spot where the body had been placed.

Chief Goodson estimated that the distance from the Silver Bucket Bar in Daytona Beach was twenty miles and that the travel time would be thirty to forty-five minutes. In cross-examination, Pearl and Goodson established several points. No one knew if the body was moved prior to discovery. It could not be established if water was always in the ditch. When identifying the Turnbull Road site, it was passed three times before Stano identified it.

Goodson was excused and Carl Clifford was called and sworn. Direct examination by Nixon established Lt. Clifford as a member of the Volusia County Sheriff's Department and that he was in charge of the Susan Bickrest investigation in December 1975. He testified that he and several other officers were dispatched to the Moody Bridge over Spruce Creek to recover a body floating in the water. Clifford explained the exact location of the bridge and how the recovery of a missing shoe on the shore established where the body had been left. Water level marks on the bridge indicated that the tide could have caused the body to float from its original resting place near the bridge.

Nixon then introduced as evidence two pictures showing the bridge, the bank of Spruce Creek, and the shoe. These established the murder scene. Finally, Lt. Clifford reported retracing the route from the address where Stano confessed to have picked up Susan Bickrest and then on to the murder site. The distance was 17.4 miles and the travel time was twenty-five minutes at a reasonable speed.

When Pearl had no questions for Clifford, he was excused. Judge Foxman then declared a ten-minute recess. When court was reconvened at 2:04 P.M., the final witness, Sgt. Paul Crow was called and was reminded that he had been previously sworn.

Nixon established that Paul Crow was a Daytona Beach police officer and that he knew Gerald Stano. After Crow identified Stano in the courtroom, he testified that he had investigated the Mary Kathleen Muldoon and Susan Bickrest cases. As part of those investigations, he brought records from his files that Nixon had marked as evidence. For the Bickrest case he provided a City of Daytona Beach Waiver of Constitutional Rights form RE: Susan Bickrest, a transcript of an August 15, 1982 confession and the cassette tape of the actual recorded confession marked "Defendant Gerald Stano, Victim Susan R. Bickrest." For the Muldoon case, he provided the standard waiver of rights form dated October 8, 1982 and a two-page, handwritten confession by Gerald Eugene Stano, dated October 8, 1982, regarding the death of Mary Kathleen

Muldoon.

During testimony, Crow explained the exact procedure for completing the Waiver of Rights Form. First it was read to Stano then it was discussed with him paragraph by paragraph, and finally it was completed by Stano writing in four questions and his name.

Pearl moved that the waiver form and confession for Bickrest be admitted as evidence without additional discussion. Judge Foxman agreed that in the previous hearing, Stano admitted that they were freely and voluntarily executed. Judge Foxman then stated: "Let the record indicate that he's (Stano) shaking his head now and saying yes."

Pearl continued, "No question had been raised concerning the voluntariness of the confession, nor the waiver of rights obtained by Sgt. Crow and no such objection will be made today."

Judge Foxman pointed out that no jury was present for the bifurcated proceeding on that either.

Nixon moved that the documents be admitted for Muldoon's case also. This was done without objection. After the evidence was marked and admitted in both cases,

Nixon insisted that the court should listen to the twelve-minute tape. Pearl reminded the court that a full and complete transcript was in evidence and that listening to it now was a waste of time. Finally, at Nixon's insistence, the tape was played in court.

Pearl cross-examined Crow. He asked him if Stano had been questioned repeatedly on the Bickrest murder, and if his memory had been "refreshed." Crow responded that the tape and transcript were very long because he had no knowledge of where the body was found. He did not have a Sheriff's Department Investigator with him, and he wanted to be sure the total territory was covered.

Next, Pearl and Crow discussed the voice volume on the tape where Crow's voice was loud and Stano's voice was softer. Crow explained how a single microphone had to be turned alternately to record the interview with each of them on different sides of the table.

Crow testified that Stano was cooperative and truthful in his confessions. He also agreed that he would not have been prosecuted or convicted in either the Bickrest or

Muldoon cases without his confessions. Crow also agreed that it was generally true that he could not have been convicted of any of the murders to which he confessed without his confessions to them.

State and defense both said they had no further evidence to present for the sentencing phase. After a discussion between counsel and Judge Foxman, it was agreed to admit the psychiatric reports as an attachment to the Presentence Investigation report. The PSI was admitted with the limitation that it would not be used to establish any aggravating circumstances. The PSI could be used by the judge for mitigation purposes only.

Judge Foxman instructed Nixon and Pearl to present their closing arguments on Friday morning. After their arguments, the judge announced that he would sequester himself and make the decision over the weekend. "My practice in capital cases, no matter what the sentence may be, life or death, I don't feel that it's fair to the defendant in the case to take a long time to do it. I hope to give you a decision and sentence, Mr. Stano, Monday afternoon at 4:00."

Court was recessed for the afternoon and

reconvened the next morning, Friday, June 10. Pearl had two motions to present to the court. First, he moved for entry of a judgment that Stano be sentenced to two life sentences based upon the fact that the evidence conclusively shows that the mitigating factors outweigh the aggravating circumstances. This motion was denied. Second, Pearl addressed his pending motion entitled "Motion to Preclude Imposition of the Death Penalty." The motion contended that the defendant could not be sentenced to death in these two cases because in so many similar cases he received a lesser sentence. Also, the motion attacked the constitutionality of the death penalty statute. These motions laid the groundwork for future points on appeal.

Judge Foxman clarified the fact that there was no deal with the state or the court at the time of sentencing on the first three homicides that would govern any other homicide at a later date. Pearl agreed that Mr. Jacobson, the attorney in the first case, made it clear that there was no deal that a life sentence was promised in any future case.

Nixon started his closing argument, ". . .

If Gerald Stano is not placed on Death Row, I believe that no murderer belongs there, the simple fact that these multiple murders and random murders of these two young women presents to the State unspeakable evil, and I believe society has a right to defend itself in requesting the imposition of the death sentence."

He then systematically related the evidence presented to establish the facts required to prove the four aggravating circumstances in each case. Often he used Stano's own confessions to show intent or the nature and character of the actions. He provided the judge with copies of other cases and rulings supporting his interpretation and application of the facts. Nixon emphasized that there was absolutely no provocation by the victims in either case.

In his argument for no mitigation, Nixon pointed out that the psychiatric evidence was clearly on the side of the State. He argued that the nonstatutory mitigating circumstances deserved little if any consideration in these cases.

Pearl stood to present the closing argument for the defense. He looked down at his notes and his angular frame appeared bent from the weight of the task before him. He opened by stating that the mitigating circumstances not only outnumbered but outweighed the aggravating circumstances established by the State. One aggravating circumstance was uncontested, that Stano had previously been convicted of six capital offenses. All other statutory aggravating circumstances had not been established, he argued.

First, the State did not meet the heavy burden of proving its case beyond and to the exclusion of every reasonable doubt. Second, if the circumstances were susceptible to more than one hypothesis, and one version was consistent with innocence, that interpretation must prevail due to the presumption of innocence. Pearl continued that it was the defendant's contention that the felony claimed in each case must be established by proof independent of the defendant's confession. The State's only indications of such felonies came from their interpretation of statements made by Stano in his confession. What he said was susceptible to more than one interpretation. Although the State claimed his statements established a kidnapping, Pearl argued that another equally valid interpretation was that he was simply trying to keep the girl in the car to convince her to engage in consensual sexual activity.

Pearl also claimed that the medical testimony did not support the aggravating factor that the murders were especially heinous, atrocious, or cruel. The victims were not tortured and were killed quickly. Unless the State could establish that the women were conscious, they could not prove that they had suffered. There was no proof that Stano attempted to drown the victims. Since the women were probably quickly rendered unconscious, Pearl argued that the murders were not especially heinous, atrocious, or cruel.

The defense argued that there was no evidence to support the aggravating factor that the murder was committed in a manner that was cold, calculated, and premeditated. Pearl claimed that the evidence established that Stano did not plan their deaths. Pearl reminded the court that Dr. Ann McMillan detailed Stano's early years, and claimed that this evidence was a mitigating factor. Pearl also claimed that Stano's confessions and guilty pleas were a mitigating factor as it saved countless hours in trial time and thousands of dollars in resources. Stano's confessions relieved the victims' families of uncertainty and demonstrated that Stano took responsibility for his actions.

Finally, Pearl argued that Stano should receive life sentences for these murders because they were no worse than the prior six cases where Judge Foxman had imposed life sentences. If Stano had confessed to the Bickrest and Muldoon murders two years ago, he would have received life sentences. Pearl argued that Stano now faced the death penalty simply because he had a bad memory. Should Stano be killed now because he forgot to tell about these two murders in 1981? Pearl claimed that to sentence Stano to death in these two cases was disproportional to the sentence he received in the prior cases.

Judge Foxman thanked both counsel for good arguments. He announced that sentencing would occur the following Monday at four o'clock in the afternoon.

On Monday, June 13, 1983, all of the principals returned to the Volusia County Courthouse Annex in Daytona Beach for the sentencing hearing. The tension was palpable. All present wondered whether Judge Foxman would sentence Stano to life in prison as he had done in 1981, or if Stano would finally receive a sentence of death.

Judge Foxman entered the courtroom and announced the two cases before the court. "Let the record reflect that Mr. Stano is here in person being represented by Mr. Pearl of our public defender's office, and that Mr. Nixon represents the State of Florida." Initially, the judge denied the defendant's motion to preclude imposition of the death penalty. Judge Foxman ordered the deputies to bring the defendant before the bench with counsel. Stano and Pearl stood in marked physical contrast. The court asked the defense if there was any legal cause to preclude sentencing, to which Pearl replied negatively. Pearl did want to make further remarks before sentence was pronounced, however, and was given permission to proceed.

Pearl asked the court to consider that Gerald Stano would never be a menace to society with the minimum mandatory sentences he was now serving. He would not be eligible for parole until he was over one hundred years old. Pearl also suggested that Stano's life should be spared because he was an appropriate subject for clinical study, and research might aid science and the criminal justice system in determining how to predict and identify psychopathic murderers.

Judge Foxman thanked Pearl and offered an opportunity to the defendant to address the court. Stano replied that he had nothing to say. Nixon also declined further comment.

"All right," the court replied, "I have a couple of observations to make, Mr. Stano. This case is different than the other homicides I've seen because of the sheer number of convictions before Florida circuit courts. This is number seven and number eight.

"As best I can tell, there are no connections between these murders; they don't involve connected defendants and this is the eighth conviction in a Florida circuit court of you for first-degree murder.

"The sheer magnitude of that number is hard to comprehend. I can see no motive for the killings, Mr. Stano. They seem to be completely senseless to me. Normally we see lust, passion, greed, a need to eliminate a witness, but I don't see that here. These murders are completely senseless. Finally, I detect no remorse whatsoever, no remorse for the two murders in front of me.

"As to case number 83-188-CC, State of Florida versus Gerald Eugene Stano, you, Gerald Eugene Stano, being now before the court attended by your attorney, Howard Pearl, having entered pleas of guilty to the offense of murder in the first degree and on March 11, 1983, having been adjudicated of said offense by this court, and you having waived your right to have a jury impaneled for sentencing and this court alone having conducted an evidentiary sentencing hearing in this cause, what have you to say why the sentence of the law should not be pronounced on you?

"Saying nothing, it is the sentence of the law and such is the judgment of this court that you, Gerald Eugene Stano, be delivered by the Sheriff of Volusia County, Florida, with a copy of this sentence forthwith to the proper officer of the Department of Corrections, and by him safely kept until by warrant of the Governor of the State of Florida you, Gerald Eugene Stano, be electrocuted until you are dead. May God have mercy on your soul."

The crowd gasped and buzzed. Newspaper reporters ran for the door to call in the news.

Judge Foxman then repeated the sentence verbatim for the case involving Mary Kathleen Muldoon. Foxman found that the State had proved all of the aggravating factors that Nixon had argued. The court found only the nonstatutory mitigating circumstances outlined by Dr. McMillan of a bad infancy and failed marriage. As required by law, Foxman weighed the aggravating and mitigating circumstances and concluded that death was the appropriate sentence in each case.

Pearl requested that the judge sign orders appointing the public defender's office for the appeals process. Judge Foxman declared Stano to be indigent, and appointed the public defender for appeal.

Court was adjourned after the brief hearing. Stano stood stunned and silent. Sentence was pronounced so quickly and with such finality that he could hardly comprehend it. Many thoughts flooded his mind. Stano said all along that he wanted to be treated and released or else receive the death penalty. Now he had been condemned to die. Florida State Prison would be better on Death Row, but for how long? In finally having to face the near term possibility of death, his reaction was predictable. He just didn't want to believe it.

Shortly afterwards, Stano told news reporters that he was surprised at the sentences of death handed down by Judge Foxman. His fellow inmates were not surprised. They had told him what to expect. Before the sentence, his lawyer had initiated forms to appeal a death sentence. Pearl warned Stano of the likelihood of death sentences in both cases. Even though Stano got what he wanted, a death sentence, and even though everyone had told him that would be the result, now that he had been actually condemned to die, Stano had the same uneasy feeling of being trapped that his many victims experienced. It was too late to turn back now.

Twenty-four

September 1983

Back at the Florida State Prison, Stano was reassigned to Death Row. The death sentences drew new media attention to his long list of confessions, convictions, and pending trials. Local and national reporters made new demands for interviews and information.

Jerry quickly settled back into the prison routine. Soon after his return to administrative custody, he was contacted by his appointed defense team from Brevard County where his next court appearance for the murder of Cathy Scharf was scheduled. Scharf was from the Daytona Beach area in Volusia County but since her murder had taken place in Brevard County, he would be tried there.

Stano's defense team, with his concurrence, offered the prosecution a guilty plea in the Scharf case in return for a no death penalty

216

plea bargain agreement. The prosecution refused, and the jury trial was scheduled. Stano was moved to the Brevard County jail for the convenience of his defense team, and the trial began.

Titusville is approximately forty miles south of Daytona Beach, but the two cities are worlds apart. Titusville is more of an inland city, a pleasant rural town. It is situated along the Indian River and Intercoastal Waterway, but it is separated from the ocean by Merritt Island and the Banana River. More important, it is due west of Cape Canaveral and the Kennedy Space Center. Many acres of marsh and space program activities have spared Titusville the carnival beach atmosphere of Daytona to the north, and has also limited ocean access.

The Brevard County Courthouse is characteristic of Titusville. It is a small, white building with large Colonial style columns, an American look found in hundreds of small towns. The jurors that would be drawn here would have a more stable, conservative small town view.

The courtroom is on the first floor. It lacks windows and is decorated with heavy, dark wooden furniture that made those present feel uneasy. Judge Gilbert Goshorn, presiding at the trial, was a smart looking, middle-aged man. His receding hairline was balanced by heavy eyebrows and glasses. A neatly trimmed beard framed his face above the black robe. His manner and bearing projected control. Jury selection of nine men and three women was completed on Monday, September 27, 1983.

On Tuesday the trial followed a pattern well-known to Stano by now, although everything seemed to take longer with a jury. Lawyers and judges had a procedural rhythm. The pace in this trial was slowed to insure that the jurors understood the significance of each step. Stano was enjoying the new experience for a change, although he rarely displayed emotion. His only signs of nervousness were chewing his fingernails and tugging at his ear.

After the identification of the case and introduction of the defense and prosecution teams, the plea was given as not guilty and the groundwork of the case was begun. The prosecution traced the disappearance of Cathy Scharf, the intensive search and finally the discovery of her skeletal remains by hunters over two months later. The facts were established by sheriffs' reports, dental and autopsy reports, and her parents' painful testimony.

Unfortunately for the State, the time interval between the disappearance and discovery of the remains made it impossible to positively establish the cause of death. Assistant State Attorney Dean Moxley wove a tale that showed "foul play" as the cause of death. Public Defender James Russo argued that the State failed to show a murder. Judge Goshorn felt that all of the facts together showed sufficient evidence that death was caused by the criminal agency of another person, which allowed Stano's confession to be introduced into evidence.

The turning point in the trial came on Wednesday. The jury had heard no shred of evidence linking Stano to the death of Cathy Scharf. The prosecution moved to enter his ten-minute taped confession as evidence. The defense team objected strenuously and tried to have the tape ruled inadmissible. If the taped confessions were not allowed in evidence, the defense felt confident that they could win an acquittal.

After lengthy discussion, Judge Goshorn ruled the confession was voluntary and admitted the tape into evidence. As it was played for the jury, spectators inched forward in their seats. Occasionally they glanced at Stano, who turned away from the jury and recorder. As all present listened to Stano talk with Sheriff's investigator Johnny Manis on the tape, most of the unknown details were filled in. Occasionally laughing and joking in the interview, Stano's voice on the tape provided details on clothes, jewelry, time, and locations. Shock registered on faces when he told of the ride and the stabbing/choking murder after which he washed his hands and went roller skating. Assistant State Attorney Dean Moxley argued, "Stano wasn't relating fiction. He put you right there in the car."

Thursday, September 30, the defense was to present their case. Before they called their witnesses, Judge Goshorn cleared the jury from the room to hear the testimony of the witnesses to rule on whether the jury should receive the evidence.

St. Petersburg Police Detective James Kappel testified that in Pinellas County, "Stano led officers to the murder scene, but failed to provide specific facts that would tie him to the killing." In that case, another suspect was arrested and was scheduled to stand trial in November. Stano admitted, then later retracted, his involvement in a second Pinellas County murder.

Dr. Fernando Stern testified that Stano may confess to things he had not done. The defense was attempting to portray Stano as a publicity seeker, a man who would confess to crimes he had not committed in order to win attention.

Judge Goshorn ruled that the Pinellas County officer was presenting opinion, and it was not pertinent to the Scharf case. In the case of Stern's testimony, the judge ruled that it had no evidentiary value since Stern could not state with reasonable medical certainty that Stano erroneously confessed to the Brevard killing. The judge disallowed the two witnesses' testimony, and so the jury never heard it.

After this ruling, the defense team decided to present no witnesses rather than a weakened defense. Another advantage gained by presenting no defense witnesses was that the defense was permitted to give the first and last arguments to the jury, with the prosecutor's closing argument sandwiched in between. Attorneys always want to have the last word. In his closing argument, Public Defender Russo attacked Stano's confession and tried to show inconsistencies, such as hair color, no stab cuts in the blouse, and no proof of death by stabbing. Alan Robinson, representing the State, reminded jurors that Stano provided details only he could know. He argued that the death had Stano's signature and urged the jury to use their good judgment. The case went to the jury, much earlier than expected, late on Thursday morning.

The jury met for five hours on Thursday afternoon. During the afternoon, they requested to view evidence. The jury finally retired at 9:00 P.M. They met again and deliberated all day Friday. During Friday, they advised the judge that after many votes they were deadlocked. The judge requested each juror to review their position and try again. At 6:45 P.M., Friday, the jury deliberations ended and Judge Goshorn declared a mistrial.

Public Defender James Russo and his assistant, Ken Friedland, considered the mistrial a victory. Stano showed absolutely no emotion after facing his first jury, and his attorneys said that he was neither happy nor sad. Assistant State Attorney Dean Moxley called the mistrial "an exercise in futility." He vowed that the State would retry Stano within the ninety-day time limit. Moxley predicted it would be difficult to seat another jury in Brevard with the widespread media attention.

The defense attorneys characterized a retrial as a waste of time and money.

The next two weeks brought a flurry of activity. The State scheduled a second Stano jury trial on November 28, 1983. Prosecutor Moxley said that anyone who questions the State's decision for a second trial does not understand that the other two death penalties could be overturned on appeal. The first jury vote was reported at 11 to 1 for conviction. Moxley considered this a mandate to try again for a jury conviction.

A series of motions were presented to Judge Goshorn from the prosecutors and defense attorneys regarding the second trial. On Monday, October 17, 1983, Judge Goshorn agreed to move the second trial to another location. After listening to arguments from both prosecutors and defense attorneys, Goshorn agreed that media reports of the taped confession presented to the first jury would prevent a fair trial in Brevard County.

Judge Goshorn told news reporters that, "I had no alternative. Rather than risk a reversal on appeal, I felt it was safer to go along with the defense and the State."

During the hearing, the judge also granted a motion from Public Defender Ken Friedland to have Stano undergo a neurological examination. According to the attorney, the multiple murderer may suffer from brain damage, and if convicted, that evidence could be presented to the jurors during sentencing.

The judge denied a series of other requests. Mr. Friedland lost on a request for a second suit of clothes for the defendant and a motion for direct acquittal. Mr. Moxley was refused his request to have the medical examiner testify that the Scharf death could have resulted from foul play. Moxley was also denied the opportunity to present testimony to the jury concerning the Maher case because of its similarity. Under Florida law, if two crimes are so similar that they suggest a modus operandi, the evidence of the other crime can be admitted.

When no courtroom was available in Fort Lauderdale, Judge Goshorn ordered the November 28 retrial moved to Jacksonville. Legal posturing continued to be reported almost daily in the newspapers.

Moxley requested permission to use John and Edith Scharf's transcripts from the first trial. He claimed that they were unavailable to testify due to the trauma it would cause them. The judge ruled that it was too early to declare the Scharfs unavailable and that there was no proof that their testimony would cause them mental or physical harm. He said that he would reconsider the State's request before the trial began.

The first week in November the State announced a new prosecution witness for the second trial, Clarence Zacke, one of Brevard County's most well-known criminals. Stano had confessed in detail to Zacke while they were cellmates. Zacke, forty-five, had been convicted of three murder-for-hire schemes, including one to kill State Attorney Douglas Cheshire. Prior to scheduling his testimony, Zacke passed a lie detector test administered by the State Attorney's Office.

Public Defender J. R. Russo began a series of moves to offset this new witness. Subpoenas were issued for State Attorney Douglas Cheshire, Melbourne Police Detective Rhuben McGee, and Satellite Beach Police Chief Tom McCarthy. Russo said, "I can't think of anything more impressive than to have the chief law enforcement officer in the circuit testify against the State's star witness to say he has a bad reputation for truth and veracity."

On Friday, November 18, Russo asked Judge Goshorn to transfer the trial back to

Titusville. The judge said that he wanted to talk to Stano on Monday before ruling on the request. Russo conceded that he was "taking a calculated risk" by returning to Brevard County, but he felt it a risk worth taking since Brevard residents were familiar with Zacke. Moxley said he would try the case anywhere that the public defender wanted.

On Monday at a hearing, Stano told Judge Goshorn that he "agreed" with the decision to move the trial back to Brevard. Judge Goshorn warned that the move might backfire since the State could reconsider calling Zacke to the stand.

Later Russo said, "It will be difficult to get a jury anywhere in the state who doesn't know Stano. Stano has gotten negative publicity here, but there has also been some positive publicity for the defense. The same jurors who know about Stano's first trial, also will know a hung jury." The trial was returned to Titusville.

The next day, Judge Goshorn issued a gag order which forbade attorneys, witnesses, law enforcement officers and court officials from discussing the upcoming trial with reporters. In the motion, the judge indicated further publicity was cited by the court as the culprit responsible for the second trial being moved to Jacksonville and then back again to Brevard. Officials said if attorneys are unable to impanel an impartial jury Monday then the proceedings still could be transferred to Jacksonville.

On Monday, November 28, jury selection for the second trial began in the Brevard County Courthouse in Titusville. Six prospective jurors were tentatively agreed upon, and State and defense agreed to try again Tuesday. Judge Goshorn talked to John and Edith Scharf in a brief hearing on Monday and excused them from testifying again. He did tell them that everyone was sympathetic, but if there was a conviction he was sure that their failure to testify would be a point raised on appeal. He warned that it could result in a guilty verdict being overturned. Despite his warning, the couple remained adamant in their refusal to take the witness stand again.

On Tuesday, a jury of seven women and five men was seated, and the second trial began. The testimony and facts established were identical to the first trial through the playing of Stano's taped confession. Then the State called Clarence Albert Zacke to the stand.

Zacke told the jury that in the summer

while he and Stano were in Brevard County jail the two talked in the exercise yard. He related Stano's story of picking up a girl named Cathy as she hitchhiked on the highway. He said he drove her to a wooded area on Merritt Island and tried to kiss her. When she told Stano that he was repulsive, he hit her and stabbed her a few times, and then he choked her.

Zacke quoted Stano: "He said when she (Scharf) would go limp, he would turn loose and she would come back to life. When she would come back to life, she begged him not to do it no more, but he would choke her again. Stano said you've got to pace yourself."

During cross-examination, Russo attempted to discredit Zacke by bringing out that for testimony in previous trials Zacke's own sentence had been cut in half. For testifying in this trial, the prosecution had agreed for Zacke to serve his time locally rather then at Florida State Prison and had agreed to return a confiscated truck to Zacke's wife.

Russo planned to discredit Zacke further by putting State Attorney Douglas Cheshire on the stand to attack Zacke's reputation. The jurors were taken from the courtroom while Judge Goshorn listened to Cheshire's testimony to weigh its pertinence to the trial. Although Cheshire had been a Melbourne resident for more than thirty years, his knowledge about Zacke came from other people. He only met the man once. The judge disallowed Cheshire's testimony saying it was inadmissible. The defense did not call any other witnesses.

On Friday morning, both sides presented their closing arguments. Assistant State Attorney Alan Robinson focused on the three confessions and details provided by Stano that only he could know. Robinson acknowledged "differences, but not conflicts" in the three confessions. The State defended the use of Zacke's testimony and labeled it "vintage Stano."

Russo, Stano's attorney, attacked all three confessions saying they were conflicting and contrived. "Which, if any, do you believe?" he asked. "Anybody can confess to something, but the test is whether the confessions match the facts in the case." The defense strongly questioned the testimony of Clarence Zacke, a convicted felon. Russo reminded the jurors that they would think about this case the rest of their lives. Had the State proved a case? "The verdict should be not guilty based on the facts and evidence you heard," he concluded.

The jury took less than three hours to return a verdict. Wearing his now familiar powder blue leisure suit, Stano glared at each of the jurors as they attested to the decision of guilt. This was Stano's ninth conviction for first-degree murder, his first by a jury. As usual, Stano showed no emotion when the jury foreman read the verdict.

On Monday, December 5, 1983, the jury heard over five hours of testimony and evidence in the sentencing phase. Gerald Stano took the stand briefly and described himself as lacking discipline and parental guidance as a child. He characterized himself as "a victim of circumstances." Stano claimed to feel sorry for his victims, their parents, and the couple who adopted him. His testimony was calm and detached. Stano refused to divulge what he had done with various murder weapons.

The defense team entered the medical reports by the various experts that had examined Stano in the last three years. The State characterized his list of crimes, the lack of any legal provocation, and the cruel aspect of this crime and the other murders he had committed. The jury was sent home and instructed to return at 9:00 A.M. on Tuesday.

After just an hour of deliberation, ten of the twelve jurors recommended Stano receive his third death penalty. Only a majority was needed in the sentencing phase, unlike the unanimous vote required in the guilt phase. On December 9, 1983, Circuit Judge Gilbert Goshorn sentenced Gerald Eugene Stano to his third death penalty for the murder of Cathy Lee Scharf. The judge found four aggravating and no mitigating circumstances. At this point, Stano was allowed to plead guilty to the murder of Sandra DuBose in exchange for a life sentence.

Another case had been progressing concurrently with the Brevard Scharf case. A Seminole County grand jury voted on October 28, 1983, to indict Stano for the November 1974 murder of "Madame X," an unidentified victim found near a shopping mall in Altamonte Springs. Stano had confessed to the slaying in October 1982. The judge entered a plea of "not guilty" for Stano during the November 16 arraignment between the first and second Cathy Scharf trials. He scheduled the "Madame X" trial for December 19, 1983.

In a plea bargain, Stano pleaded guilty and waived a jury trial before Judge Robert B. McGregor. In turn, he received his eighth life sentence on January 13, 1984. Officials believed this was the first time in Florida that a person had been indicted, found guilty, and sentenced in the slaying of an unidentified person. It was the second time Stano had confessed to the murder of an unidentified female in court.

On January 15, 1984, Stano was sent back to the Death Row at Florida State Penitentiary in Starke. Stano would never face another murder trial. He entered Death Row with three death sentences and eight life terms from murder convictions in five different Florida counties for the deaths of fourteen women. Although he confessed to many more, no other cases were tried, nor is it likely that they ever will be. Stano was where he belonged and where he wanted to be.

Twenty-five

Few people, especially the victims' survivors, understand why the appeals system in death penalty cases takes so long to complete. This dissatisfaction is felt by many observers of the criminal justice system. In the September 3, 1985 decision of that court in the case of another Florida death-sentenced inmate, Willie Jasper Darden, then Chief Justice Burger wrote to express disagreement that the court was accepting Darden's case for review: "In the twelve years since petitioner was convicted of murder and sentenced to death, the issues now raised in the petition for certiorari have been considered by this Court four times . . . and have been passed upon by no fewer than ninety-five times by federal and state court judges." The court accepted the case, issued a decision in which Darden lost again, and he was executed on March 15, 1988, almost fifteen years after the murder was committed.

In Florida, in cases after the death penalty is imposed, there are two phases of appellate review. The first tier is the direct appeal. To save time, the state intermediate appellate court is bypassed, and the case is sent directly to the Supreme Court of Florida. The appellate rules set time limits for each step in the process to insure the appeal reaches the State Supreme Court in a reasonable time. Extensions of the time requirements can be requested and are granted when justified. Cases involving trials can comprise thousands of pages, and court reporters often need more time to transcribe the record.

During the June 13, 1983 sentencing phase of the Muldoon and Bickrest cases, Stano's lawyer requested that a public defender be appointed for the appeals of the two death sentences. Judge Foxman found Stano was indigent, and appointed the public defender to represent him on appeal at the county's expense. The case was quickly assigned to Christopher Quarles, the Capital Appeals Division Chief, in the Public Defender's Appellate Division. The Muldoon and Bickrest cases were consolidated for appeal.

The purpose of the direct appeal in the Supreme Court of Florida is to examine the trial record and rule on possible errors by the judge. Legal rulings on evidence and objections and the court's findings in support of the death sentence are reviewed. To provide the record to the State Supreme Court, Quarles notified the clerk of the circuit court and the court reporter to begin preparation of the record and transcripts. All of the exhibits and transcripts are assembled and transmitted to the appellate court.

After the record was filed in the Supreme Court of Florida, Quarles filed a written brief on January 3, 1984. This initial brief presented his arguments for reversing the circuit court's decision. This was less than one month after the cumulative time prescribed for all activities since sentencing. Quarles filed his brief on time despite the fact that his ability to see Stano was limited. Stano was then deeply involved in the two Brevard County Cathy Scharf trials, and in the "Madame X" proceedings in Seminole County.

The Florida Attorney General's office quickly answered the initial brief with the State's arguments for affirming the judgment and sentence. Quarles then filed a reply brief, trying to refute the State's position. Once all the briefs were filed, the appeal was completed and could be set for oral argument before the Supreme Court of Florida.

In his appellate brief, Quarles argued that the death sentences in the murders of both Muldoon and Bickrest cases were improper for several reasons. He claimed that the trial court improperly imposed the death penalty and erred in denying his motion to preclude imposition of the death sentence. Comparing these two murders to the prior six for which Stano had received life sentences, Quarles claimed that the facts of the current cases were no more compelling than the murders where Stano received life sentences. The same prosecutor, the same judge, the same circumstances were present in 1981 and 1983, therefore, Stano should be sentenced to life imprisonment for these murders as well. The State responded that the prior life sentences were imposed pursuant to a plea bargain, whereas in 1983 there was no deal, thus making the death penalty an appropriate penalty.

The brief also argued that the court improperly used the same facts to establish two aggravating circumstances, failed to find valid mitigating factors concerning mental capacity, and incorrectly sentenced Stano to death. Quarles emphasized the higher credibility of

Dr. McMillan's diagnosis based upon her extensive examination of Stano. The State cited to the judge's sentencing order which found facts to support each aggravating factor. The decision is for the trial judge to make, claimed the State, and the sentences imposed in this case were in accordance with Florida law.

The Supreme Court of Florida unanimously rejected all of Stano's arguments and affirmed the judgments and sentences of death in the Muldoon and Bickrest cases on November 1, 1984. Quarles moved for rehearing, asking the court to reconsider the ruling, which was denied on January 13, 1985. On February 19, 1985, The Supreme Court of Florida reaffirmed its decision to be final.

The last step in the direct appeal process is to petition the United States Supreme Court to accept review of the case. If federal constitutional claims are raised in a final decision of the highest court in a state, the U.S. Supreme Court may agree to accept review of the case to ensure that the State court has properly interpreted the federal Constitution. Such petitions are routine in capital cases because federal constitutional rights are always implicated. Claims are alternatively phrased as due process violations, and the sentence is alleged to constitute cruel and unusual punish-

237

ment. However, the U.S. Supreme Court accepts review in less than one percent of the cases where petitions for writ of certiorari are requested. Stano's case was no exception. Although Quarles filed his petition for writ of certiorari, the State filed an opposing pleading, and the Court declined to accept the case for review by order dated May 13, 1985.

The direct appeal process in the Bickrest/Muldoon cases was completed in less than two years from the imposition of sentence.

The second Scharf trial resulted in the imposition of the death sentence on Stano on December 9, 1983, almost exactly six months after the Bickrest/Muldoon sentences. Quarles was again appointed to represent Stano in his appeal to the Supreme Court of Florida. The Scharf appeal followed the same procedural path as the Bickrest/Muldoon case, with the second case lagging about six months behind at every step.

In the Scharf appeal, Quarles had more to work with after a trial instead of a confession by guilty plea. He argued that the trial court committed several errors in admitting or not admitting evidence, and claimed that the State's evidence failed to prove that Cathy Scharf's death was caused by the criminal agency of another person, as opposed to natural causes. The death sentence was attacked by claiming that the aggravating factors the judge found were not supported by the evidence, and by claiming that the mitigating factors of diminished mental capacity were ignored. The State responded that the judge's evidentiary rulings were correct and that the sentence was in accordance with Florida law.

On July 11, 1985, the Supreme Court of Florida affirmed the conviction and sentence of death for the murder of Cathy Lee Scharf. Quarles again moved the court to reconsider its ruling, which was denied on September 4, 1985.

A petition was filed in the United States Supreme Court, where Quarles claimed that the State Supreme Court failed to honor Stano's federal constitutional rights. The high Court declined to consider the case by order dated January 23, 1986. At this point, the direct appeals in both cases were finished, and the second tier of State review began.

Under Florida law, the second stage of review of a criminal conviction requires the claims to be filed in the trial court within two calendar years of the direct appeal becoming final, or from the denial of the United States

239

Supreme Court to accept the case. The review raises claims that were not and could not have been raised on direct appeal.

The public defender system in Florida only provides legal counsel to indigent defendants through the direct appeal system. In most criminal cases, the defendant represents himself from that stage on. Defendants on Death Row have more at stake, however, and courts are reluctant to allow an execution of someone who is not represented by an attorney. In 1985, the Florida legislature recognized that Death Row inmates needed legal counsel and created the Capital Collateral Representative (CCR) to provide legal representation for any person convicted and sentenced to death who is unable to secure counsel due to indigency. This guarantees that the defendant can seek review in a competent and timely manner, and assures the citizens of the state that the judgments of the courts will be reviewed, then promptly carried out.

Stano was one of the first Death Row inmates assigned a lawyer from the new CCR. Stano's new lawyer was one of CCR's best, Harvard educated Mark Olive, whose intelligence and wit had earned him a formidable courtroom reputation.

Although the appeals process was of greatest interest to Gerald Stano, his participation was limited. Defendants are not present at appellate proceedings, and Stano waited in his cell on Death Row for the outcome of his appeals. Other inmates schooled him on the intricacies of the appellate system, and his frequent contact with his attorneys kept him informed.

Apart from the judicial review process is the clemency review. The governor, through his clemency board comprised of the five cabinet secretaries, has the authority to grant mercy and commute a death sentence to life in prison. A Brevard County attorney, Sam Baxter Bardwell, was appointed to present Stano's case to the clemency board. He argued that Stano's life should be spared so that he could be studied as a serial killer by psychiatrists.

On May 22, 1986, Governor Graham denied clemency and signed a death warrant directing the superintendent of Florida State Prison to cause Stano's sentence of death to be executed for the murder of Cathy Lee Scharf. Execution was scheduled for July 2, 1986. Just four months into the two year time limit for filing appeals had passed in the Scharf case since the direct appeal became final. The state was shortening Stano's review schedule by expediting his appeals process.

The Brevard County Circuit Court Judge, anticipating the motion, and realizing the limited time available for review after a death warrant is signed, made numerous calls to Mark Olive urging him to file the motion as soon as possible. Delay is the defendant's main tactic in death warrant cases, however, because if the case cannot be reviewed in the hours before the death sentence is to be carried out, the court will be forced to grant a stay of execution so that a thorough review of the claims can be made. Olive predictably failed to comply with the trial court's request for an early filing. He filed the motion with the trial court less than twenty-four hours before Stano's scheduled execution. Judge Gil Goshorn held a hearing that afternoon on the two-hundred-page motion.

The hearing opened with the judge formally noting the presence of Stano, Olive, his trial attorneys, Russo and Friedland, and Margene Roper, attorney for the State. Margene Roper found a unique niche in the Attorney General's Office specializing in prosecuting death penalty cases under warrant. After ten years

of practicing law, she thrived on the excitement of the precedent-setting cases she argued
at every level of the state and federal court
systems. At this level of legal practice, the
maneuvering is much like a game of chess,
and Roper was a consummate player.

Of the several claims presented in the motion, Judge Goshorn recognized only the
claim of ineffective assistance of counsel. The
court asked Olive to proceed with the hearing
since the prior defense attorneys were present
and available as witnesses. Olive asked for additional witnesses, and more time to compel
their presence to support his claim of trial
counsel's substandard performance, but the
judge refused. Roper announced that the state
was prepared to proceed with an evidentiary
hearing on the ineffective assistance of counsel claim. Reluctantly, Olive agreed to proceed, but conceded that he could not prevail
without the witnesses he desired. Olive was
taking a calculated risk to try to force the
court to stay the execution scheduled the next
morning. His gamble lost. When Judge
Goshorn heard this concession, he ruled that
it was foolish to proceed to a full hearing on
a claim that counsel agreed he could not
prove. The court denied an evidentiary hearing and denied the motion. Olive was uncharacteristically speechless.

Immediately after the ruling, Olive filed a notice of appeal in the Supreme Court of Florida to secure review of the summary denial of his earlier motion. With only hours to spare, the Supreme Court of Florida granted a stay of execution so that it could review the case. The death warrant expired.

Florida's death warrants are active for only one week. When the execution is scheduled on the last day of the warrant week, there is nothing to encourage the defendant to rush to file his last round of legal challenges. When any court needs more time to review the issues, even a day or two, the stay effectively nullifies the warrant because it expires on its own terms before the court can consider the issues.

On October 16, 1986, after full briefing by both parties, the Supreme Court of Florida issued its decision affirming Judge Goshorn's order of summary denial of the motion for collateral relief. They held that Olive had foregone the right to present evidence when he conceded that he could not prevail. Olive sought review by petition in the United States Supreme Court, which was denied on May 18, 1987.

As soon as the Scharf case became embroiled in the appeal, Governor Graham signed a death warrant in the Bickrest/Muldoon case on November 6, 1986. The warrant was active for the week of November 26 to December 3, 1986, which included the Thanksgiving holiday. Stano's execution was scheduled for December 2, 1986.

Racing to the wire, Olive filed his appeals motion in Volusia County on Sunday, November 30, 1986. To achieve every tactical advantage over the State's attorneys, Olive filed the motion in the clerk's office by special arrangement, but delivered the forty-pound package of his motion and supporting exhibits to the attorney general's office by bus in an attempt to further delay the process. Late Sunday night, the motion was in the hands of the State's attorneys, and they began preparing their response.

The next morning, December 1, 1986, Volusia Circuit Court Judge Foxman conducted a hearing on the thousand-page motion. He decided that more time was needed to fully consider the voluminous claims, and granted a stay of execution. This was the second time that Stano had been less than a day from his death.

Judge Foxman, relieved from the pressures

of the death warrant, set a schedule for the State's formal response to the allegations in the motion. A hearing was scheduled after all parties submitted their written arguments on April 9, 1987.

At the appointed hour, Judge Foxman entered and routinely dispensed with opening formalities. He called the case, and noted the presence of CCR attorneys Olive and Lisa Gardner, as well as the attorneys for the state, Roper, Assistant State Attorney Ray Starke, and Assistant Attorney General Belle Turner. The court instructed Olive to argue his claims.

First, Olive claimed that defense counsel in the Bickrest/Muldoon cases was ineffective for not challenging the confessions and permitting the guilty pleas upon which they were based, and claimed that Pearl had a conflict of interest from representing Stano on the first six murder cases. Olive alleged that there had been a conspiracy between Crow, Stano's parents, Dr. McMillan and Stano's attorney to force Stano to confess falsely to crimes he did not commit. Olive noted that the only evidence against Stano came from his own mouth. Olive insisted that an evidentiary hearing was necessary to develop and prove these claims.

After a brief recess, Belle Turner argued for the State. She had only been an attorney for a few years, but her intelligence and legal ability made her a rising star in the Attorney General's office. Turner was assigned tough cases like Stano's because she always presented the State's best case and usually won. She claimed that the law was clear that any inquiry into the confessions was waived by the guilty pleas, which are in effect an in court confession of guilt. Even if the confessions were subject to attack, she argued that the time to raise that issue was on direct appeal, and since Stano had missed this chance, he was now procedurally barred from bringing this claim.

The main thrust of the State's case was that Pearl had done exactly what Stano insisted: proceed to enter guilty pleas without delay. Pearl had stated that his discovery and investigation was incomplete, but Stano himself insisted on proceeding immediately. It was reasonable for Pearl to conduct no further investigation and accede to Stano's demands. To refute the claim that Stano was a serial confessor and not a serial murderer, she pointed out that Stano confessed to anyone who would listen, when any alleged coercion was nonexistent and Crow was nowhere around. Stano had reaffirmed his confessions to the jury in Brevard County, and to his cellmates. Turner argued that even if Pearl could have done more, Stano could not establish that he was prejudiced such that the outcome of the proceedings would have been different. In summary, the State saw no need for an evidentiary hearing because the record established that the pleas were valid and all the remaining claims were procedurally barred.

The following week, Judge Foxman denied the entire motion without a further hearing. Olive appealed the denial of the motion to the Supreme Court of Florida. After appellate briefs were filed, the court issued an opinion on February 25, 1988, affirming Judge Foxman's order. The two step review in state court was now complete.

Twenty-six

Another death warrant was signed in the Scharf case on June 4, 1987, with execution scheduled for August 26. The only avenue of review available to Stano now was in the federal court by petition for writ of habeas corpus. One of the oldest legal actions, a writ of habeas corpus literally means "produce the body," and orders the head of the state corrections system to explain why a prisoner is being detained in violation of his federal constitutional rights. The federal habeas corpus review examines questions of federal law that have been presented to the state courts before, and rejected. The federal reviewing courts are the final arbiter of federal law, and the writ is the vehicle for state prisoners to obtain review of their claims in federal court.

At 8:00 A.M., on August 22, 1986, just a few days before his scheduled execution, Olive filed an enormous petition for writ of habeas corpus asking the United States District Court to stay the execution and grant relief. On August 23, the State filed its response to the petition, which was prepared in anticipation of the claims Stano would raise in federal court. United States District Court Judge Patricia Fawcett conducted a limited hearing on the petition on August 23 and 24, at the Orlando division of the court.

To complicate the review process, Olive reiterated his position that all of Stano's convictions were invalid because of the "conspiracy" to get Stano to confess falsely. Olive contended that each of the convictions, life and death sentences, were all inextricably intertwined. Complexity was created with the number of cases and the myriad of issues and witnesses attendant to them all. Under this broad premise, interrogation techniques in the Maher and Van Haddocks cases in 1980 would be used to invalidate an unrelated conviction years later in the Scharf case. The defense claimed to need over one hundred witnesses at the evidentiary hearing, and requested federal marshals to fan out over the entire country to serve subpoenas at the expense of the State.

Roper and Turner argued that the claims were barred, and no hearing was necessary. Judge Fawcett decided to entertain testimony on the one claim of alleged ineffective assistance of counsel, and permitted testimony from Russo and Friedland. Within a few hours of the hearing, Judge Fawcett dismissed the petition by order dated August 25, 1987, just hours before the scheduled execution.

Olive immediately filed an appeal with the Eleventh Circuit Court of Appeals in Atlanta.

That court gave Stano a stay of execution from seven in the morning to one that afternoon. After entertaining an oral argument on the stay, the court granted a permanent stay of execution that afternoon. Stano had won a few more months of life. After nearly three years, the Eleventh Circuit issued an opinion in the Scharf case, sending the case back to the District Court for a limited evidentiary hearing. Judge Fawcett scheduled a new Scharf hearing for September 1991, over four years after the same claims had been rejected in the August 1987 appeal.

Following the Supreme Court of Florida's denial of relief in the Bickrest/Muldoon case in 1988, a second death warrant was immediately signed by the governor on April 27, 1988. The execution was scheduled for the week beginning noon, May 18, 1988.

On May 10, Olive filed a series of motions seeking further review in the Supreme Court of Florida, which were all denied by May 16. The same day, Olive returned to Judge Fawcett and filed another petition for writ of habeas corpus in the United States District Court. She conducted a limited hearing on May 17 and 18, before issuing a forty-two-page decision denying Stano all requested relief. Later that day, the eve of execution, the Eleventh Circuit granted a permanent stay of execution to consider the appeal. The three judge panel issued a decision invalidating the guilty pleas. The court ruled that Pearl's unpreparedness had the effect of denying Stano the advice of counsel, and that he was proceeding as his own attorney without the required warnings against self-representation. The court then took the unusual step of granting a rehearing before all of the judges, due to the importance of the case.

On January 2, 1991, the court reaffirmed the guilty plea issue, finding that Pearl's representation was reasonable given that his client insisted on pleading guilty without delay. The case was sent back to the original panel for resolution of the remaining issues. No final decision has been announced in the Bickrest/Muldoon appeal to date.

After the August 1987 Stano appeal in the Scharf case before Judge Fawcett, Assistant Attorney General Belle Turner and others complained about the conduct of CCR attorneys in the Stano case and many other capital cases. Turner's specific concerns were the use of second party affidavits wherein a CCR investigator or CCR attorney would report conversation with possible witnesses in the Gerald Stano cases. She believed that these conversations would be presented as fact without the knowledge, review, or approval of the person being quoted.

In early 1988, Governor Bob Martinez signed executive orders directing the FDLE and State Attorney Willie N. Meggs to investigate allegations of criminal conduct on the part of CCR employees.

In their findings and conclusions, the FDLE report found that, "None of these situations involve prosecutable cases of perjury." It further stated that, "The number of allegations point out a disturbing pattern of abuse of affidavits."

Four Stano defense affidavits were examined in detail by FDLE. Three were refuted by the potential witnesses quoted, and the fourth witness swore to events that he did not witness. Other defense affidavits were not signed, such as the one attributed to Stano's father. None of this failure of proof was acknowledged by the U.S. Court of Appeals when they referred the case back to Judge Fawcett.

At 4:30 in the afternoon on Friday, September 6, 1991, in the third-floor courtroom of the Federal Building in Orlando, Judge Patricia Fawcett initiated the scheduled Scharf evidentiary hearing. She had sent specific orders to the attorneys in June 1990, detailing the preparation expected on the remaining issues before the court. She repeated these three defense claims again for the record: first that the state knowingly withheld evidence of the conspiracy; second, that there was such a conspiracy between Crow, Jacobson, McMillan and Stano's parents to get Stano to confess to crimes that he did not commit; and third, the alleged illegal use of prisoner Clarence Zacke as a State witness.

Judge Fawcett acknowledged that there were a

number of motions before the court from both sides. Before ruling on these motions she stated that she wished to question the legal representative of Gerald Stano. Mark Olive slowly rose. His appearance had changed significantly. He seemed pale, thinner, and physically drained. His responses were slow, very measured, and barely audible. Several times he was asked to speak up so that the court reporter could hear him. He looked nervous and worried. Twice while Judge Fawcett asked direct questions, he sat down to compose himself before answering. Judge Fawcett questioned Olive on the challenged affidavits. Olive quickly replied that they would all be signed.

Stano's defense team had not complied with Judge Fawcett's order in the fifteen months provided. Mark Olive admitted under her intense questioning that he was not prepared and had accomplished little other than speaking to six or seven potential witnesses. He acknowledged that he was the attorney for Stano, but under a new and strange set of circumstances.

Some time after the August 1987 appearance in District Court, and before the Eleventh Circuit ordered the Scharf case to be reheard, the Stano defense team of Mark Olive and Lisa Gardner stopped working as Capital Collateral Representatives. During the questioning, Mark Olive was reluctant to discuss his current relationship with CCR, their absence in court, or CCR's written motion to withdraw from the case. He repeatedly stated that he could not speak for CCR. Olive was also requesting federal payment for his representation of Stano and federal payment for the investigators and experts he needed to prove his case. He claimed that CCR would not pay him or help in Stano's defense.

Judge Fawcett instructed both counsel that there would be a conference telephone call between the judge, Mr. Spaulding, chief of CCR, Mark Olive, and Assistant Attorney General Margene Roper. Judge Fawcett reluctantly granted Olive's motion for a delay and postponed the hearing until January 22, 1992. The judge gave the State permission to move for summary judgment in the case by November 1, 1991. She also directed that CCR would remain as cocounsel and would assist Olive with his investigation. He was directed to notify the court within ten days of the type of experts needed and for what specific purpose.

Although the State was ready to proceed as instructed by the judge, they were again prevented from finishing Stano's appeals. The State did file a motion for sanctions against Mark Olive for unreasonable delay which the court took under consideration. Mark Olive asked several times if he should have a lawyer, and expressed difficulty working under this threat. Court was adjourned until the January hearing.

At the Scharf evidentiary hearing, an interesting development occurred in the Bickrest/Muldoon cases. In the appeal of the death sentencing involving a murderer named Roy Harich, his defense claimed that Public Defender Howard Pearl worked for the Sheriff's Department as a special deputy. If true, this would be a conflict of interest.

Howard Pearl, like many other lawyers and judges who deal with persons involved in serious crimes, felt a need to have a weapon for personal safety. A quick and easy way to carry a weapon legally was to be appointed as a special deputy sheriff. This practice was well-known, but had never been challenged before.

The United States Court of Appeals in Atlanta granted Harich's motion, and remanded the case all the way back to the state court for a hearing on the motion. This first test case found that Pearl's defense was not prejudiced and the judgments were upheld. However, it was also ruled that each case must have an individual hearing to determine whether Pearl's status as a deputy sheriff prejudiced the individual defendant's cases. Mark Olive moved to amend the claim to include it in the Bickrest/Muldoon appeal, which was granted. It and several other Howard Pearl cases were remanded back to the state court for a hearing. This decision included the Bickrest/Muldoon cases.

Twenty-seven

January 1992

The federal trial court in Orlando is situated about one hundred yards west of Interstate 4. The highway is elevated through the downtown area, and parking for the United States District Court is in the area under the Interstate. It is a metered parking area that requires ten quarters at one time for all day parking.

Early in the cool morning of January 22, 1992, it was amusing to watch the participants in the Stano evidentiary hearing arrive from out of town. Downtown Orlando would not awaken for at least another hour. No one dared to be late in Judge Fawcett's court, and that was a real possibility since few had the required number of quarters. Someone found a change machine at the Metro Bus Terminal one block south and two blocks east, and, grumbling about the meter inconvenience, the cast assembled in the third-floor hallway outside the courtrooms waiting for the drama to begin.

Mark Olive had issued subpoenas to almost every participant in the Stano murder trials. Each mahogany bench in the corridor was filled with judges, lawyers, doctors, and law enforcement personnel from a wide area of Florida's east coast. Many present had made career changes since their involvement with Stano's case. Former prosecutor Dean Moxley was now a circuit court judge, Sergeant Paul Crow was now Chief of Police, some had retired and others had left law enforcement all together and moved to other states. Attorney Jacobson had joined the Public Defender's office and was accompanied by his attractive new wife. Dr. McMillan was present as well.

There were pockets of nervous, manufactured conversation about all subjects except Stano and the conspiracy claim to be heard today. The defense team arrived with three hand trucks stacked with at least four file boxes each. The box ends were stamped with "Pro life" and "Stamp Out the Death Penalty" stickers. A retinue of young CCR investigators and assistants nervously hovered around Mark Olive as he checked the inventory of materials and gave last minute instructions.

The doors to Judge Fawcett's court were closed and a sign on a pedestal announced that court was in session. A federal drug case had run over from yesterday, and the short sentencing phase was taking place. Finally the doors were opened, and the participants in the evidentiary hearing slowly entered and positioned themselves. Margene Roper and Barbara Davis were representing the state. The two tall women were dressed in business suits. The younger, Davis, was a crisp contrast to the more experienced but rumpled Roper. Davis was trim, tan, and athletic. As if prosecuting capital cases was not enough competition, Davis spent her weekends participating in triathalon competitions, running, biking, and swimming. Several medals adorned her office. Davis and Roper began unpacking their own voluminous materials and arranging them in their projected order of use, by witness and by case.

As everyone waited for this final hearing to begin, Paul Crow thought about his testimony in Washington, D.C. on death penalty cases. Before a congressional subcommittee, he spoke of a handful of renegade attorneys that he felt had really impeded the criminal justice system. "It has nothing to do with individuals," he had said. "It has to do with life or death. That is their real zest, their focus, their interest. Once you understand that you can come to grips with the deceiving things that they do." This characterization perfectly fit today's zealous defense team.

"What frustrates me as the ditch digger," Crow confided later, "is the reality that I've smelled the body. I've looked the mother and father in the face. I've gone through the emotional windmill. And all of a sudden you end up in an air-conditioned, perfumed courtroom in Orlando and everybody has a $500 suit on. It is a totally different setting, and you are arguing over totally different values. The victims and secondary victims (parents and friends) are forgotten."

In spite of all the notoriety and acclaim Paul Crow had received in the Stano case, he had a personal frustration with it. "It was as if the damned thing turned and came back at me." He knew what had been said about his investigation and how the newspapers had repeated the allegations. For years he was frustrated as people wrote and reported news stories about the case yet never asked him directly about his viewpoint. Crow wanted his day in court.

"I had to prove something," he said. "I had to prove my credibility. In law enforcement you must have unquestionable integrity and credibility. If you lose them, you lose everything."

Stano was brought to the defense table in leg irons by two corrections officers from the court prisoner holding cell. As soon as he was seated, Stano looked around for familiar faces and smiled in recognition. He looked neat in his light yellow shirt and dark rimmed glasses, but the effect of eleven years in prison ages a man, even Stano.

Judge Fawcett immediately entered from her

chambers. Standing at the foot of the bench, she conferred briefly with the bailiffs and court clerk, then she took her seat on the bench and proceeded in her crisp, controlled manner. Judge Fawcett has long fingers and she takes notes constantly on a yellow legal pad. When she is not writing, she pivots the pencil forward in her hand and uses it like a baton to punctuate her point. During the proceedings, she often prompts the attorneys and witnesses from her detailed notes.

Mark Olive, dressed in a well tailored dark suit, took two cardboard file boxes from the defense team area and set them on the rail of the empty jury box. This was the only surface near him that was not filled with file boxes.

The first witness he called was Officer James Gadberry, Jr., of the Daytona Beach Police Department. Olive claimed in court briefs and orally that Gadberry was representative of many officers who were unwilling to publicly express their concerns about the Stano case for fear of retribution. Gadberry was Olive's cornerstone for building a case that Crow was feeding Stano data for confessions for personal glory.

Gadberry was above average height, well proportioned with a medium build, and his countenance seemed deliberate. Noticeably balding, he wore a mustache and spoke softly. His testimony was, at best, confusing. He first testified that

Donna Hensley's wounds were superficial in a picture he saw and that he had personally seen them after they healed. On cross-examination, he admitted that he had no personal knowledge of the wounds but knew that stitches had been required. In his 1980 arrest report, he stated that Stano knew circumstances of the Maher murder that only the murderer would know. Today his testimony was that Stano reacted only to prompting by Crow and stated that, "Stano agreed to whatever questions were put in front of him."

Gadberry could not recall crucial information concerning the trip to the Maher crime scene such as the time of day, number of police vehicles, and who drove. Gadberry also said that he did not get out of the car. Several other officers present contradicted him and testified later that they did leave the cars to walk around. Gadberry did not observe the route taken nor did he know if Stano was giving directions to the location where the body was recovered. He could not even recall specifics about the crime scene.

Under cross-examination, Gadberry stated that he did not voice his concerns until Stano was sentenced to death in subsequent cases. He testified that the department was under pressure to solve the Maher case at the time, a statement which Captain Powers, his chief at the time, said was untrue.

After his testimony, spectators did not know which Gadberry version to believe. His testimony was, in fact, a weak beginning to the hearing.

The second witness called was Carl Stephen Lehman. Lehman had been a deputy sheriff in Volusia County, Florida, and had participated in the Van Haddocks case. Now he lived in Pennsylvania.

His testimony involved the Van Haddocks confession and the agreement between prosecutor Larry Nixon and defense attorney Don Jacobson that Stano would receive a life sentence for crimes committed in Volusia County and the Seventh Judicial Circuit. Van Haddocks came under this umbrella, subsequent cases in other jurisdictions did not. This witness covered no new information in the case.

Olive had repeatedly tried to include all Stano confessions after the Nixon-Jacobson plea bargain agreement as part of that agreement. Larry Nixon did not have the authority to cut a deal on crimes committed outside his jurisdiction. The complicating factor was that Stano picked up some girls up in Daytona Beach, then drove to another county or circuit for the actual murder and disposal of the remains.

Next an articulate Lawrence Nixon took the stand. He made it quite clear from the beginning of his testimony that he would not dance to Olive's tune. Nixon's career since graduation from the University of Florida in 1971 had been quite remarkable, and his intelligence and courtroom expertise was well-known. Though slightly built and unusually pale skinned, his physical appearance in the dark blue suit with a distinguished graying beard embodied confidence. Olive tried repeatedly to extract a yes or no answer to questions. Nixon calmly insisted on detailed answers to make his response perfectly clear. He would rub his high forehead before slowly responding with several interpretations to Olive's questions.

Nixon testified that Stano was never offered life in prison in exchange for confessions to all murders he had committed. This clearly eliminated Olive's counterclaims. Olive was never able to establish any unusual relationship or collusion between Nixon, Crow, Jacobson, and McMillan with this witness.

Olive was trying to put a new interpretation on previously recorded actions and to prove an alleged conspiracy. The witnesses were not saying what Olive had said their testimony would be in his list of witnesses filed with the court. He was beginning to show signs of frustration in his conduct and in his questioning. Things were not going well for him.

Terrell Walter Ecker, a mild-mannered free-lance reporter, took the stand and branched off into a totally new area. He said that for twenty-five years he had been a writer and journalist and at one time considered writing a book about the Stano case. He said he had a literary agent also, and had talked to Crow several times about this effort but neither had felt comfortable writing about an ongoing case. Ecker was interested in the investigation techniques, and he had a series of talks with Crow thinking that he would add "color" to his book. A brain aneurysm in April 1982 ended his writing career.

When witness Martin M. Markowitz was called, he identified himself as a trained technician in tape analysis. He testified that he could determine whether a person was being truthful on a tape through his analysis. He was of the opinion that the Maher confession tapes by Stano were rehearsed scripts and not freely given confessions.

Margene Roper conducted a very brief cross-examination for the State. The judge finally held that Markowitz's testimony was beyond the competency of alleged electronic stress analysis. Stano had confessed the Maher murder to many people. This testimony did not suggest or establish that Crow was feeding information to Stano as Olive and his defense team now were trying to prove.

On the second day of the hearing, the first witness was Eugene Stano, Gerald's father. He was a small, sad man, almost bald, and deeply tanned. He was professional in appearance, and his manner was calm and polite. In response to questions from Olive, he told of three brief meetings with Jacobson and McMillan and one at which Crow was included. Mr. Stano removed his horn-rimmed glasses to wipe away tears as he spoke of encouraging Jerry to confess to additional crimes. He looked at his son sadly and expressed regret at having encouraged him to confess. It was a dramatically emotional scene. This was a rare moment when Jerry also showed sadness or possible remorse in the courtroom, if not for his victims then at least for the effect of his crimes upon his own family. Under cross-examination, Stano stated that no one had asked him to have Jerry confess to crimes that he did not commit or falsely confess to, but just to tell the truth.

Dr. Ann McMillan was the next witness. The psychologist wore a tailored dark blue suit, open neck red blouse, and her graying hair was short with bangs. She wore clear glasses, but changed to bifocal sunglasses to read from boxes of notes. Her slow, deliberate manner upset Olive. He would shiver with quiet impatience and nervously run his fingers through his collar-length hair as Dr. McMillan consulted one day-timer after another. She constantly referred to these old diaries for answers to questions about meetings or dates which occurred over ten years ago.

Her testimony quickly exposed the weakness of the conspiracy claim. She testified that she hardly knew Paul Crow, and saw him only three times briefly. She totally dismissed any suggestion that she instructed Crow on how to interrogate Stano. She declared that Crow's training in this area far exceeded hers. Dr. McMillan had copies of newspaper articles misquoting her, and she specifically repudiated the articles as untrue and unreliable. She stated that it was not her impression that Crow and Jacobson were working together. If testimony is a battle of wits between lawyer and witness, this witness won.

As Paul Crow came to the stand, spectators in the courtroom sat up attentively. After Crow introduced himself for the record, his account of the activities involving the Stano series of confessions began. Crow often paused before answering questions. On several occasions Crow stated that he could not state the date but could fix the time of a meeting in relation to other events in order to establish approximate dates. Judge Fawcett often interrupted the questioning of Crow by Olive to clarify the events being discussed and to pinpoint the length and subject of conversations between Crow, McMillan, Jacobson, Nixon, and Lehman. His testimony was consistent with McMillan's account of their three brief meetings. His testimony was very detailed, except for some dates, and the longer he stayed on the witness stand the more obvious it became that he was telling the truth. Judge Fawcett took many pages of notes during his testimony. It would be easy to cross-check Crow's statements by referring to previous testimony and records.

His lengthy testimony continued over a period of five days.

On Thursday, Olive tried to discredit the validity of Stano's confessions by pointing out the lack of attack weapons in evidence and the confusion over the kind of knife used. Crow stunned everyone in the courtroom when he reached in his briefcase and said, "I have the knife right here." Bailiffs jumped and the hearing was interrupted while Judge Fawcett determined just how a witness could bring a knife through building security and into the courtroom. Crow's briefcase obviously was not checked by security since he was a known police officer. Judge Fawcett gave the head bailiff new instructions for tighter security.

To Olive's astonishment, Crow produced a chart showing locations of the girls Stano had killed. He said the chart had been created to demonstrate the close proximity of the cases. For instance, the murder of Mary Carol Maher and the Hensley assault were within the same block in Daytona

Beach. It reflected all reports of crimes against women in the boardwalk area. Crow discovered that several women had accused Stano of assault and battery after being picked up in this area. There were open missing person reports or criminal investigations involving Ramona Neal, Debra Jackson, Donna Hensley, Mary Carol Maher, Hazel Allen, and Patricia Courtney. When Crow contacted Dave Hudson of the Volusia County Sheriff's Department for help, Crow added the names of Linda Hamilton and Nancy Heard.

Early in the case Crow thought Stano was a possible serial killer. This chart demonstrated why he came to this conclusion. Olive was livid about the use of the chart during Crow's testimony. It showed a strong pattern of Stano activity, some previously not introduced in court. It reinforced Stano's confessions as valid. Judge Fawcett asked Crow to explain the chart in detail.

"The blue dots survived Stano attacks," he said, "the red dots did not. Dot 5, Debra Jackson, is the important one. She was a live victim. She said she was picked up at the Holiday Inn Boardwalk by Stano and taken behind a church. After she took her clothes off, she was asked to perform oral sex. Stano reached under the car seat, and she jumped out of the car and ran. She called the police from a house on Halifax Avenue.

"Stano drove back to Main Street and was stopped by police. Her clothes were in his car. She was brought to Main Street, she identified him,

269

and then she didn't want to prosecute him." Debra Jackson was the first to identify Stano, but Donna Hensley was the first to be willing to prosecute him. The chart tied the whole case together, and illustrated Crow's thought process twelve years earlier.

During this period, Crow described his relationship with Jacobson as at arm's length. They were not working together or even sharing information. Jacobson and McMillan had characterized Stano as a short-term killer. Crow firmly disagreed. When Crow had mentioned his suspicion to Jacobson that Stano had killed more than one or two women, Jacobson had said, "Prove it. Show me!"

During the period from April 1980, when Stano confessed to the Maher murder, until September 1981, when Stano entered a guilty plea to six Volusia County murders, Crow and Jacobson (and Jacobson's investigator, Warren Walker) did not exchange any reports, photos, or data in murders where Crow suspected Stano. Crow did supply to Jacobson very limited information such as body location to identify possible Volusia murder victims when he was instructed by Nixon to do so, *after* the plea bargain was made. Crow was cooperating with the prosecutor, Nixon, in a proper manner.

The function of Paul Crow in the Stano cases

outside his jurisdiction was clarified by Crow, and confirmed by the testimony of others, as that of a conduit. When he received information from Stano about a victim from another jurisdiction, Crow would refer the information to them. The defense claim that he supplied Stano the details for his confessions was exposed as impossible since Crow did not have access to the data.

Most importantly for Paul Crow, the rumors of his collaboration on a book and defense charges that he obsessively sought personal glory were finally and properly put to rest. Crow's interest in any book was a text to be used to train law enforcement people in the investigation of serial killers and the problems of cases covering many jurisdictions. Crow's testimony removed this taint of speculation and innuendo from the record.

Ken Morrison, Florida Department of Law Enforcement, Tallahassee, Florida, was now called. He had worked on the FDLE Task Force which investigated the Stano Florida murders in areas outside Volusia and Brevard counties. His testimony again was not as Olive had represented it would be. Morrison did state that he had heard Stano and Crow talk about a book, but did not know if they were joking or serious. His testimony regarding the access to Stano was routine. The defense team had repeatedly claimed that Crow kept others from having access to Stano. A series of witnesses including Morrison and Mr. Eugene Stano denied this claim.

Nancy Jacobson, Don Jacobson's former wife, was called to testify. Although her manner on the witness stand and testimony did not indicate good feelings toward her former husband, she said nothing to support Stano's claims. She specifically had no recall of Don Jacobson having interest in writing a book.

After a week of testimony, the third member of the alleged conspiracy, Stano's original defense lawyer, Don Jacobson, was called to testify. His testimony generated great interest because until Jacobson was discharged by Stano, he had been prevented from revealing information about his relationship and knowledge of Stano. What he had to say surprised everyone, even Paul Crow.

Mr. Jacobson identified himself for the record as a former FBI investigator, an experienced criminal attorney in several capital cases, and a former attorney for Stano. He stated that on April 1, 1980, Stano called him from the jail and made a murder confession to him. He interviewed Stano several times, and Stano confessed to the six murders in Volusia County and other murders as well. Jacobson hired an investigator, Warren Walker, to determine if Stano's confessions were truthful or if he was falsely confessing. He hired Dr. Ann McMillan to perform psychological tests on Stano.

Jacobson testified that he had determined through independent investigation that Stano had in fact committed the murders that he had confessed to.

The defense claimed that confession data flowed from police records to Crow to Jacobson to Stano, who then confessed. Everyone now knew that Stano originated the murder data to Jacobson prior to the plea agreement with Nixon and months before Stano confessed the murders to Paul Crow. Significantly, five of the six murders in the first Stano trial did not happen in Crow's jurisdiction, and other offices controlled the records. Stano clearly knew about the murders before Paul Crow, and he had told his attorney about them. Mark Olive had disproved his own claim by having Jacobson testify.

Jacobson described his relationship with Paul Crow as one of adversaries up to the plea bargain agreement with Nixon. He testified that the very limited information he obtained from Crow's investigation only confirmed what Stano had already confessed to him. Jacobson did not ask Dr. McMillan to determine if Stano was a serial killer because he had determined that through investigation. Although Jacobson had known Crow since 1966, their relationship was through limited professional contacts, not personal. He knew Crow was a graduate of the FBI school and did not request Dr. McMillan to instruct Crow on how to interrogate Stano.

Jacobson said that in his confessions to him, Stano knew details that only the killer of these women could know. From the beginning, Stano and his parents begged Jacobson to pursue a defense plea of insanity for Jerry. Jerry feared the death penalty. His parents could not accept that their son committed these murders. Jacobson had Stano evaluated by two doctors in Gainesville in order to establish a plea of insanity. When Jacobson was able to get the agreement with Nixon, the insanity defense was not continued. Jacobson said that he spoke in terms of insanity to Stano's parents out of compassion.

Jacobson, the defense attorney, described his relationship with Nixon as professional. They had been adversaries in previous legal cases. Because Jacobson knew that Stano was guilty, he pursued the plea agreement with Nixon. His testimony and Nixon's agreed on the limitation of the agreement to bodies of victims found in the Seventh Judicial Circuit, Nixon's jurisdiction. Jacobson testified that he made that clear to Stano on several occasions and that Stano understood if a body had not been left within the area under the agreement that Stano was not to talk about it to the authorities. He emphasized this since Stano had confessed murders to Jacobson outside the agreement area. Jacobson advised Stano that these other murders were "taboo" and not to be mentioned or discussed by Stano with anyone. Stano wanted to take a lie detector test to prove that he killed the people he admitted killing under the agreement, not to prove his innocence. Jacobson refused to allow this.

Jacobson testified that he concurred that Crow be designated as the person to obtain information concerning the six murders in Volusia County after Stano had been given immunity. Crow was located in Daytona Beach close to Nixon and Jacobson, and it reduced the administrative load for Nixon and Jacobson. Crow served as a member of Nixon's prosecution team.

Donald Jacobson testified that he had no interest in writing a book, and he had never taken any action toward writing one. Stano wrote to Jacobson concerning a possible book.

Although Jacobson knew Crow had been approached by several people about books, Crow never indicated that he would write one. Jacobson said that rumors about Crow doing this became a source of jokes. A humorous greeting to Crow would be, "Well, how's the book going?"

Jacobson's testimony, when combined with Crow's, Nixon's and McMillan's indicate that Stano had very good early representation. He would have probably escaped with life in prison for six murders if he had not been such a compulsive talker and braggart. He was a victim of his own mouth, not of a conspiracy.

The next witness was Johnny L. Manis, Cocoa, Florida. Mr. Manis identified himself as a former Brevard County Homicide Detective in the Sheriff's Department. He had not been in law enforcement since 1984. Manis related that he was assigned to the Scharf case by Lt. James Bollick of the Brevard County Sheriff's office in response to a request for an investigation from Sgt. Paul Crow in Daytona Beach. Crow wrote Manis a letter dated November 20, 1981 and they talked by telephone. Manis testified that in a November or December 1981 telephone conversation, Paul Crow did not state to Manis that he had a confession from Stano.

On January 20, 1982, Manis and Lt. Bollick visited Stano at the Florida State Prison. Stano was friendly, but Stano told Manis that he did not recall any crimes in Brevard County. When Manis returned to Brevard County, he advised Sgt. Crow of the lack of results from the visit. Crow responded that Stano only would talk to people if he liked them.

After two or three telephone calls between Crow and Manis, Manis advised Crow that he would like to question Stano again about two victims, Sandra DuBose and Cathy Lee Scharf. In April, Crow drove to the prison, and Manis and Bollick flew. Crow had arrived first and met the Brevard men on his way out. Crow advised Manis that

Stano insisted on being transported back to Volusia County before talking to anyone. All three men returned home.

After a court order, Stano was returned to Daytona Beach jail on August 10, 1982. Manis testified he visited the jail on August 11, 1982, to see when he could be scheduled to talk to Stano. He was not prepared to interview Stano since he did not have his case files or recorder, but when given the surprise chance to do so, he did. Crow advised Stano of his rights and Stano filled out the waiver form in the presence of Manis. Crow got the other two men coffee and asked if they wanted anything else. Stano replied that he would like to go for a jog, and everyone laughed. Crow left after a short period of time. Manis asked Stano questions for about an hour. Stano discussed both the Scharf and DuBose murders with Manis.

Manis testified that he left and returned the next day, August 12, 1982, to record Stano's testimony. He had his recorder and case files and a waiver of rights form. Manis read the Miranda rights to Stano. Stano waived his rights, and Manis taped the interview with Stano. Manis identified as true and correct the transcript of Stano's confession on August 12, 1982, the court exhibit bearing his name. Judge Fawcett could not get an answer from Mark Olive on how the copy of the Stano August 12, 1982 confession that he filed with the U.S. Eleventh Circuit Court of Appeals and the Orlando District Court showed Crow's name, not Manis's. Someone tampered with the document. During a recess at the hearing, Paul Crow asked Mark Olive if he illegally stole documents from Crow's files. Olive replied in a joking manner that he wished that he had taken more.

Next called was James A. McDonald, Jr., a former deputy in the Brevard County Sheriff's Department. He testified that he investigated the location where Cathy Lee Scharf's remains were found in 1974. At the time he was not aware of a missing person's report on Scharf in Volusia County. After he identified the victim, McDonald contacted Lt. Ouellette of the Daytona police for routine assistance about information on the victim and her actions up to when she was last seen. He testified that the case was always a Brevard County case, never a joint investigation with any agency. He did acknowledge that former Daytona Beach Police Detective Susan Nix and others were assigned by Lt. Ouellette to obtain Scharf information, but they did not work for him. McDonald also authorized the Brevard Sheriff's Crime Lab to make an intelligence bulletin. The bulletin showed the names of Brevard Sheriff's Department and other agencies, which may have had contact with the victim. These agencies being listed did not constitute a joint investigation of the Scharf case, merely where the report was sent.

The final hearing witness on Friday, January 31, 1992, was Donald Allen Denton of the Bradford County Sheriff's Department. He testified about the murder of Barbara Ann Bauer, whose body was discovered in Bradford County. Denton first interviewed Stano in Florida State Prison without success. He later interviewed him at the Daytona Beach Police Department and there Stano confessed to the Bauer murder. Stano supplied information about the murder that Denton did not know, and Sgt. Crow did not know. Denton stated that Crow never denied him access to Stano. In fact, other Bradford County representatives visited Stano on August 23, 1982, at the Volusia County Court House, without the assistance of Crow, where Stano freely confessed again.

After his testimony, the hearing was continued until further notice due to the court's schedule. Olive had used all of the time thus far and was not finished. The State would have to wait to present their case. Court was adjourned.

Twenty-eight

Judge Fawcett notified attorneys from both sides that court would reconvene on March 5, 1992. All of the principal participants were in place at the appointed hour, and Mark Olive was asked to continue. John Dean Moxley, Jr. was called to testify.

He was sworn in and identified for the record. Moxley testified that he was the prosecuting attorney in the two Scharf jury trials, the DuBose case and the case of "Madame X."

He said that he made a presentation to the grand jury in the fall of 1982 to encourage the Brevard County Sheriff to follow up on Crow's letter requesting investigation in the Scharf case. The grand jury recommended further investigation.

In March 1983, Moxley made a second grand jury presentation. This time he presented as witnesses Officers Manis, Kendrick, Hudson, and Crow plus the Brevard County State's Attorney Investigator George Dirshka. The jury issued an indictment to Stano for the murder of Cathy Lee Scharf.

Moxley personally headed an extensive investigation of the Scharf case. He and others interviewed witnesses, took depositions, and visited other jurisdictions to examine their files and to gain knowledge of Stano and how he killed others. Moxley personally checked the facts in the Stano confession to Manis. He drove the route given by Stano using an old road map. The routes taken had been redesignated since 1974, and Stano's route was correct using the designations current at the time of the murder. Also correct were Stano's description of the palm fronds over the body, the clothes being worn, and the victim's jewelry.

Moxley testified that Crow was only used as a witness in the penalty phase of the trial. He stated, "The confessions of Stano to Manis were the most important confessions in his prosecution of Stano for the Scharf murder." Moxley said that he did not consider the statement by Stano to Crow in March 1981 as the "linchpin" of his case. He had no information that Stano was promised life imprisonment for the Scharf murder. In fact, Stano himself confessed to Moxley that he murdered Scharf and DuBose and offered to plead guilty in exchange for life imprisonment. After Stano was convicted of the murder of Cathy Lee Scharf, he was allowed to plead guilty to the murder of Sandra DuBose in exchange for waiver of the death penalty.

He further testified that no one in the Scharf case had problems with access to Stano. He had no knowledge of a "conspiracy" and no knowledge of Stano being "fed" details to confess. His testimony was very positive that Brevard County independently investigated and prosecuted the murder of Cathy Scharf. He declared that Crow was not under his control, and had no role in developing the Scharf case for trial.

Since all of Olive's attempts to taint the Scharf conviction with claims of participation by Crow were fruitless, he turned to attack the Zacke confession. This was an unusual phase of the hearing due to the backgrounds and personalities involved. A respected judge was followed by colorful characters, several of whom were convicted felons.

Marlene Alva, a lawyer, testified concerning jail house sweeps in Brevard County. Melvin Shakleford, Marvin Glen Cook, and Lawrence Litus testified to Brevard County Jail rumors and conversations about "snitches" in the jail. Their testimony was related to the affidavits of Johnny Jim Mallory and Curtis David, Sr. concerning the use of snitches by Brevard County authorities. They all described a technique or method of operation but did not tie it to Stano and Zacke.

Clarence Zacke testified that he provided the information to the authorities on his own. Like Moxley before him, Zacke said that no one told him to get information from Stano. Kenneth Friedland, Stano's attorney in the Scharf trials, testified that he explored the conditions of the Zacke confession thoroughly during the second state court trial. He also stated that he knew of the plea agreement in the Hunt case before Stano's second Scharf trial where the Zacke confession was introduced. No evidence was introduced that Zacke was an agent of the State.

The most unique in this group of witnesses was William Van Poyck. After he was sworn in, he identified himself as an inmate on Death Row with Stano. He testified that he was asked by Stano to help him in this case. He said, however, that Zacke never stated that he was acting as a government agent or for the State Attorney. This witness certainly lacked credibility and had no direct knowledge about the events of which he testified.

The next witness called was Susan Nix. She knew and had worked with Paul Crow and Jim Gadberry. Nix assisted the Brevard County Sheriff's Department in 1975 when they requested background information in the Scharf case. She later went to work for FDLE where she supervised Ken Morrison, another witness, who worked on the FDLE Stano Task Force. She was a featured witness in Olive's case, but her recollection of conversations were vague and inconsistent with testimony from several other witnesses.

Judge Fawcett in her findings wrote, "The Court rejects as unreliable the testimony of Susan Nix that Crow stated to her that he was writing a book about Stano and that the more murders Crow solved the better the profits would be. Not only is Ms. Nix's recollection of these purported conversations vague, but also Ms. Nix's recollection of the facts proved inaccurate in other regards." The judge then went on to give examples of conflicting testimony.

Kathy Kelly was next to take the stand. She is a tall, gaunt, nervous woman. Her blond hair was rolled back from her face in what could be called "Andrews-Sisters-style," which made her appear even taller. She said that she had been a staff writer with the *Daytona Beach News Journal* for twenty-nine years. She testified that she had submitted several chapters of a proposed book on Gerald Stano to a literary agent, based on her correspondence with Stano, but that the project was not currently active. Kelly said Crow knew about her book attempt, but never suggested that they author a book jointly. She testified that there were many rumors about Crow and a book, and that she even mentioned the rumors to Crow.

In two weeks of testimony involving twenty-six

witnesses and several affidavits, Mark Olive had presented his claims in behalf of Stano. It did not appear to observers that the Stano team had established any new facts. In Olive's pretrial report to the court, he stated how he expected his witnesses to testify, but most of them gave contrary testimony. This concluded the Plaintiff's presentation.

The State now called a few witnesses to disprove the Stano claims. They recalled Paul Crow and Dean Moxley to clarify or emphasize specific points. One new witness called was former Daytona Beach Police Chief Captain Marvin Powers. His statements did much to strengthen Crow's testimony by discrediting Officer Gadberry. Chief Powers testified that when he first learned of Gadberry's claim in 1985 or 1986 that Stano was not guilty, he conducted his own investigation and found that Gadberry was incorrect. He further said that Gadberry was inaccurate on several points including the Maher confession, the fact that Gadberry worked for Paul Crow, and Gadberry's problem with completing his work. Powers testified that Gadberry grew to resent Crow after the success of the Stano case and the rumors of a book began.

The next witness called by Margene Roper was

John H. Gaston. On April 1, 1980, he was locking a suspect in a cell when Stano engaged him in conversation from his nearby cell. Stano gave an unprompted, voluntary confession to the Maher murder. On that day Stano also confessed to the Maher murder to Crow and Jacobson.

Roper continued to discredit Gadberry's testimony by calling Sgt. Martin J. White of the Daytona Beach Police Department. He testified that Gadberry bragged about identifying Stano and solving the Maher case in 1980. White said it was not until after Gadberry returned to the police force in 1985 or 1986 after working as a church director of youth ministries, did Gadberry change his mind about Stano's guilt. After his return, Gadberry stated that Stano was not guilty of anything and that Crow had "made it all up."

Sgt. David W. Hudson of the Volusia County Sheriff's Office gave detailed testimony regarding victims' case records, which he maintained. He testified that Crow had no access to the case details and therefore could not have fed them to Stano. He testified that Stano gave explicit information that only the killer could know and led them to remote murder scenes without prompting. Hudson told the details of the Stano confessions in the Nancy Heard, Ramona Neal, Linda Hamilton, and Jane Doe murders. Hudson's testimony made it sound impossible that Crow gave Stano information for his confessions.

Much of the work for the State had been accomplished by Mark Olive. The facts in evidence did not support Stano's claims. The hearing ended on March 9, 1992.

Judge Fawcett rendered her eighty-page decision on June 10, 1992. She denied all of the Stano claims and sent the Eleventh Circuit Court of Appeals detailed findings of fact and conclusions of law. Factual findings can rarely be reversed on appeal. There was no conspiracy, no faulty confessions, no book for fame and fortune.

After reading Judge Fawcett's order, Paul Crow remarked, "Judge Fawcett has great intuition. She was a federal judge at thirty-five. She has got to be very smart. The judge asked very pointed questions and kept everything on that yellow legal pad. I was the only uncoached witness that appeared. I played it from the hip and obviously she picked up on it."

Now that the hearing was over, everything was much clearer. Crow continued, "I didn't realize in my dumb way that Gerald would throw up on Jacobson and tell him everything. It was such a dumb deal that Stano had told Jacobson about the cases. So we had a very unusual set of circumstances. You had an attorney with a great cancer on his mind with a conscience, and he wanted to play the games and play the role. I picked up on it with Ann McMillan. I kept feeling that they wanted me to come to the table and tell them what

I really suspected him doing, and I would not do it. I kept backing away from them. I thought Stano was a long-term killer and did not agree with what McMillan and Jacobson were saying. I didn't want to get sucked into this game. I realized that Jacobson wanted me to be part of a process to make Gerald a short-term killer. I thought Jacobson went out of his way to do it. Now I realize that he was saying it on behalf of his client. Jacobson wanted to bring Stano in under the six confessions, get everything done, and forget about it. Judge Fawcett saw it," Crow concluded.

Crow also praised Judge Dean Moxley, calling him a "catalyst" in the case. Moxley had been Assistant State Attorney during the Stano investigation, and Crow admired his handling of the medical examiner in the Scharf case. "A medical examiner looked at a set of bones in a field twelve years ago," Crow recalled, "and wrote a report saying cause of death was unknown. He has looked at thousands of bodies since then, but not the old medical report. All of a sudden he is on the witness stand to testify as to the probable cause of death, and repeats 'cause unknown.' But in the second Scharf trial, Moxley asked the medical examiner if it was normal for someone to lay down in a field or swamp, put holes in her shirt, put palm fronds over her body, and kill herself. What does this give the impression of? Someone murdered her! In this way the medical examiner's testimony went from unknown causes to death by others or foul play."

Anyone who has followed the Stano trials has to wonder how the U.S. Court of Appeals could have ordered this evidentiary hearing. Mark Olive presented a plausible argument to the appellate court that Stano was a victim of a conspiracy of ambitious people who induced him to confess to murders that he did not commit. Olive claimed Stano was a serial confessor, not a serial killer. He used the affidavits of fellow Daytona Beach Officers Gadberry and Susan Nix to discredit Paul Crow. Attached as additional evidence were the inaccurate, unsigned affidavits of other case principals. Most importantly, Olive could claim that no state or federal court had ever heard of these Stano claims. Prior to considering Stano's final federal appeal, the court directed the hearing to eliminate any doubt of Stano's guilt.

Twenty-nine

The media attention to Gerald Stano's death sentences created questions about Stano and his murders, confessions, and trials. The principal question: Why did he murder?

Although only Stano's twisted mind holds the answer to why he murdered, the best professional explanation emerged in the Cathy Scharf trial. Five psychiatrists had examined Stano in his earlier Volusia County cases, but Public Defender James Russo, his attorney in Brevard County, asked for a new psychological evaluation for possible use as a mitigating circumstance to avoid the death penalty. On September 25, 1983, Dr. Gerald Mussenden, a psychologist from Tampa, evaluated Stano. The report was not introduced in 1983 because his lawyers felt it would have hurt Stano, but the report surfaced in the proceedings in Stano's effort to avoid electrocution in 1986. Dr. Mussenden administered nine psychological tests and conducted extensive interviews. Stano was extremely cooperative, open, informative, and direct throughout the evaluation and appeared emotionally controlled. He was found to be functioning in the low average to average range of intelligence without any unusual problems. He was free of any neurological dysfunctions. Stano was characterized as "well oriented to person, place and time; was in good contact with reality; was alert to his surroundings and emotionally stable." Overall, Gerald Stano appeared to be average or normal and related to others without any unusual problems.

On the question of why Gerald Stano was a serial killer, Dr. Mussenden stated, ". . . Specifically, psychological testing indicates that Gerald is a fairly self-centered individual who appears to be more preoccupied with the gratification of his own drives and desires rather than disciplining himself to be much more concerned for the welfare of others. In essence, he would rather sacrifice others for his own drives rather than sacrifice himself. In addition, he continues to be somewhat preoccupied with his own appearance. Testing also indicates that Gerald has a tendency to be somewhat defensive and quick to feel a sense of threat or rejection from others which is part of his distortive style of interaction. He is quick to perceive threat or negativistic tendencies in others and often is only perceiving what he has actually created or what is not present. In such situations he becomes extremely angry or negativistic and then quite susceptible to acting out without the appropriate controls and restraints. This is especially noticed when he is interacting with women where they are less able to protect themselves and he can feel much more powerful and controlling. Thus, his anger can be easily displaced on them and without any types of controls or inhibitions. Many of his statements throughout the evaluation indicated that he never had any concerns regarding women retaliating his physical abuse but did make statements that he would be extremely concerned if he interacted with an abusive man. Thus, he experienced no threat from women and would become abusive towards them without any second thoughts or reservations.

"Testing also indicated that Gerald is extremely dependent on the affection and support of women, although he is still extremely angry and negativistic towards them. Being so dependent on their affection, praise, and support, he becomes extremely angry when he does not receive it. In essence, he is like a child who is in constant need of the love and affection of a mother and becomes extremely upset when they lose it for any brief moment. In Gerald's case, such feelings become overwhelming and he reacts with an uncontrollable vengeance. All the women he has assaulted or killed were involved in extremely negativistic, hostile types of interactions with him . . .

"Gerald Stano was also asked questions regarding many of the murder charges he has had against him. Gerald indicated that in every case where he was charged and convicted of a murder he did have some type of negative, hostile argument with the women involved. He indicated the arguments always involved some criticism that they made towards him. To some extent it appears that he intentionally provoked these negative interactions by how he basically presented himself.

"Unfortunately, the women involved responded to his negativistic tendencies, resulting in Gerald becoming extremely angry and dangerous. He indicated that the women he had murdered in the past all criticized him in some manner which enraged him. Typical comments that most of the women made were that they did not like the way he was driving, which was the result of his weaving in the street while he was extremely intoxicated. Secondly, they would indicate that he was severely intoxicated and that they had disliked it. Thirdly, he indicated that they would dislike the music he had on his radio and possibly even disliked how loud it might have been. Next, he indicates that they also criticized the way he dressed which was a severe blow

293

to his self-concept since he felt he was an excellent dresser. In addition, it appears that he was extremely obsessive in trying to keep his car clean and resented how they would all sit in his car and dirty the floor with their dirty shoes. He also noted that many of them appeared to be somewhat verbally aggressive and were somewhat intimidating.

"As a result he would become extremely angry with them and at one point would punch them while he was driving and tell them to either be quiet or that he was going to kill them if they would say anything else. This eventually would result in the women being quiet while he continued to drive to some remote spot. Once he arrived at the remote spot he then indicated that he would take out the knife that he had underneath his seat and stab the women. In essence, this entire style would indicate that all of these murders were premeditated and that he received some form of satisfaction by attacking these women after they would verbally attack him."

At first Stano denied to Dr. Mussenden that he committed the Cathy Scharf murder, then later admitted killing her. When confronted with this contradiction, he explained that he did not want to admit to anything which might lead to the electric chair. At the time of this evaluation, he was not trying to brag; he was trying to deny charges in order to escape prosecution. In September 1983, he had no thoughts of trying to appear as a glamorized multiple murderer. He was evaluated as extremely scared of the electric chair and fighting desperately for acquittal of charges.

In summary, Gerald Stano was evaluated as well aware of what he was doing and saying. Testing indicated that he could be a reasonably controlled and restrained individual. However, according to Dr. Mussenden, he could also be extremely volatile, dangerous, and homicidal. In a chilling prediction, Dr. Mussenden concluded, "It appears that there are many other crimes that he (Stano) has committed which he has not admitted to."

The other mental health experts who examined Stano applied different labels to describe him, but the experts generally agreed that he was legally sane when he committed the murders. They all noted his lack of conscience and lack of remorse. The term "schizophrenic" was often used, indicating that Stano was divorced from reality. He was also labeled a "sociopath," indicating his hostility toward society.

These labels do not explain fully the question of why he murdered. Dr. Ann McMillan specifically addressed this question, and concluded,

"Stano was never normal. He is the closest I've ever seen to a bad seed. It's like he was born without a soul. During Stano's first six months of life, his basic needs were not satisfied. His level of survival and life support needs were more like those experienced by subhuman animals in similar conditions. Jerry has never had a conscience. Murder gave him a sense of power.

"Jerry just decided that everybody was a prostitute because it's what he wanted everybody to be, and he had some knowledge of his natural mother and that situation."

Stano's natural mother reportedly learned promiscuity within her own family as an abused child. She offered Jerry for adoption in fear that her husband would notice that he looked different and suspect that he was not the father.

Jerry first tried to claim insanity as his reason for killing. Several experienced psychiatrists and the courts have rejected this excuse saying that Stano does not meet the accepted court criteria for insanity. In fact, no judge even allowed any form of diminished mental capacity as a mitigating circumstance in sentencing. It is generally agreed that Stano knew what he was doing and did it willfully.

Stano also tried to blame his wife and their failed relationship. Anger originating with his wife was not a plausible cause. He murdered before, during, and after his marriage. His marriage counselor, Dr. Davis, flatly rejected the marriage as a cause or mitigating factor in the murders.

When questioned during his confessions on why he killed, Stano always responded by describing the critical moment or situation where his "red rage" was activated and the intense "other Jerry" possessed him and brutally murdered without remorse. In fact, his decision to kill was made much earlier, and the murder was premeditated. The victim was simply picked by chance.

Stano's confessions indicate that he was fascinated with the process of death. He used a variety of techniques including stabbing, shooting, strangulation and drowning. He was physically active in the deaths and enjoyed the excitement.

Stano boasted to Clarence Zacke that he had perfected the technique of slow death by intermittent strangulation. He seemed proud to confess to chasing Janine Ligotino and Ann Arceneaux, both bleeding from stab wounds, through a field before killing them. After his arrest, reports surfaced from several prostitutes that he had forced them to run away nude or partially clothed as he shot at them. A young college girl visiting Daytona was forced to run for her life nude. She ran terrified to a house where police were called. He was arrested, but the young woman refused to press charges. She returned to her home in the north leaving Stano free to continue killing.

Why did Stano kill? Since he had no ability to love, no conscience and related only to objects instead of people, killing seemed rational. It was a game that he enjoyed which made him feel powerful. There was no remorse because to him the lives of his victims had no meaning.

Even Stano's confessions provoked questions. Why did he confess at all? Early he confessed as part of the plea bargain. After his long sentence and confinement, he became a serial confessor for the same reasons that he was a serial killer. The confessions gave him the power, attention, and notoriety that he so strongly desired. Dr. McMillan not only predicted Stano's confessions, but explained that once confined in jail, confessing to his previous crimes was his only outlet.

How could Stano remember details so vividly for so many years? If you asked a professional golfer about his best shot in a long past golf tournament, or asked a retired baseball player to describe the winning pitch, what you'd get would be a graphic account. Stano's sport and highest level of exciting satisfaction was murdering women. Details about locations, clothing, jewelry, and his car at the time, all were indelible images which he shared with investigators.

To avoid the electric chair, Stano's attorneys claimed that he was fed the information contained in his confessions. This claim was never accepted, and is not true. In his initial confessions to Paul Crow, Stano confessed to crimes that were completely unknown to Crow. These crimes occurred in Volusia County, outside of Crow's jurisdiction in Daytona Beach. After the confessions, unsolved case files were arranged chronologically by another officer with the Sheriff's Department. Three of the first six confessions were found in the sheriff's files. No one could have given Stano this data. Victim details of location, clothing, and such were matched to these old cases. The same thing happened later when Stano confessed to the FDLE Task Force. He gave details that only he could have known, and officers tracked down verification through local officials.

In one case after giving routine information, Stano was asked if he could tell the investigator something special. Stano said, "All I can tell you is I had to scream at the woman. I had to yell at her. She couldn't hear me."

When the investigator looked at the police report, there was no reference to hearing. Checking back with her family, he discovered that she was seventy per cent deaf.

In another case, Stano said, "All I can tell you is she acted like a kid." The investigator said, "Sure. She was twenty-one years old." Stano insisted that she acted like a kid. When the investigator double-checked, he learned that the victim had been thrown from a horse. She had brain damage and acted like an eleven-year-old child.

What happened to other evidence in the cases? First, consider the casual nature of the encounters. Most women were picked up and given an automobile ride. Some were at the beach in bathing suits. Others were in bars or they were prostitutes walking the street. Stano confessed to throwing away shoes, purses, and other identifying articles left in his car. Jewelry was found on many of the victims and often their purses were nearby. Robbery was apparently not a motive.

Stano told Crow in confidence that he had put his trophies in a specific place and not to worry about them. Stano told Sergeant Jesse Blitch of the Gainesville Police Department that he had the knife that he used to stab Arceneaux and Ligotino, but would not tell him where it was hidden at that time. As their communication was restricted by Stano's lawyers, the trophies became a loose end. Crow suspects that they will be found in Tomoka State Park.

Many of the victims were strangled. When a weapon was used, it was not found; Stano said he disposed of them. At the Scharf sentencing hearing, he refused under oath to answer where guns, knives, or other mementoes might be located. Police profiles predict that serial murderers keep some personal article from each of their victims. No one knows whether Stano has a secret trophy case. Police searched Stano's room, his parents' home, and they completely disassembled his car. No evidence was found. His mother maintained that she did his laundry and that she would have found blood or some other evidence had he committed these heinous murders. Stano explained how he scrubbed his car clean after each murder. He was meticulous in his personal appearance and methodically left no traces of his acts.

His first letter from jail when he was initially arrested was to his brother asking him to "straighten up his room." Evidence was also eliminated when victims were taken to remote locations and murdered outside of the car. Most of these victims were not discovered soon enough to reveal many facts about the crime. Within several hours, the physical evidence of sexual activity is lost and no victim was found that quickly.

Did Stano always act alone? Several investigators do not think so. They will not say so in public because they have no positive evidence. Two cases in particular indicate the possible participation of a second person. In the Gainesville case, two young, healthy, active girls were murdered at the same time with a knife. In the Bradford County case of Barbara Bauer, Stano traveled a long way, disposed of her car in another state, and returned to his car in Florida. Stano even stated once that he knew people expected him to implicate others. Possibly this will be part of his final confession.

How could Stano murder for eight years and not get caught? The victims were in different police jurisdictions. During the years 1973 to 1980, Florida police records were not automated. Unsolved murders could not be cross-checked for similarities. Stano had no relationship with his victims before the murder. Often he did not even live near the victim or murder scene. The victims were not related in any way except that they were female. Many of them were leading life-styles that isolated them from their families and people who knew them. They were divorced, separated, runaways, orphans, prostitutes or strangers in town on vacation. Most importantly, Stano appeared to be an average person who worked at routine jobs and did ordinary things.

This is one of Paul Crow's favorite topics. "People are naive to the fact that murder is one of the easiest crimes to get away with because of Florida's climate. A body left in the woods, two hundred yards off of the road, will skeletonize in two weeks due to the heat, humidity, and animal activity. A second point is the car. It is my impression that as soon as they have their driver's license the killing spree starts. Mobility is their big cover."

How did Stano choose his victims? No one but him knows this for certain, but some facts are known. Most of the women got into his car willingly. All but the two in Gainesville were alone when he picked them up. The majority were picked up at night. Almost half of the victims were picked up with the intended purpose of obtaining sex. The rest either had car trouble or were hitchhiking.

Over ninety percent of Stano's victims wore blue. Early theories placed great significance on this fact. Was this because blue denim was popular at the time? Psychiatrists suggested blue was chosen because it was his adopted brother's favorite color and that Stano was expressing hatred for him. Opposing this theory are his memories of Claudia. Once during a presentence investigation report, Stano spoke at length about his relationship with Claudia, a girl from Pennsylvania with whom he had his most serious relationship. Back in his room after he had killed, Stano said that Claudia would appear to him in a vision wearing the same blue pantsuit that she had worn on their first date.

Those who have studied Stano's murder pattern believe that the act of murder was premeditated but that his victims were selected randomly. The victims were unfortunately at the wrong place at the wrong time when they met him.

Was Stano a mass murderer, or a serial killer? Most enforcement professionals consider mass murderers as people who murder a large number of victims at one time in one place. They are usually violent and acting a rage. Charles Manson killed seven persons during two nights in August 1969. He is a mass murderer. Serial killers commit single murders over and over again, with days, weeks, or months separating the killings. These are people who fit easily into everyday life and have no conscience and no remorse for acts of violence. Albert DeSalvo, the "Boston Strangler," killed eighteen women between 1962 and

1964. He was a serial killer.

Stano is a textbook example of a serial killer. He murdered for at least eight years and had over three dozen random victims. He was withdrawn, mild mannered, had few friends, and was involved with music. He was ridiculed by classmates and victims, and he could not hold a job. He strangled or stabbed most of his victims, but did shoot some after being assaulted by one victim. Stano was captured by accident on an assault charge, not for murder. He confessed to over thirty murders after his arrest. Stano looked at his time out of prison with investigators as a vacation. He has shown absolutely no remorse. The fact that he was caught at all was a rare combination of luck and circumstance.

Even Paul Crow agreed that there was a large measure of luck. Luck is often defined as what happens when opportunity meets preparation. Crow described it this way. "I use this dumb phrase: seldom does a person having a heart attack walk into a heart surgeon's office. That is rare. That is basically what happened in a stupid way." Paul Crow's unique training in the recognition and investigation of serial killers was indeed rare in 1980.

Crow classifies killers in two groups: organized and disorganized. He explains that a disorganized killer is one that probably has psychological problems and kills in a residential neighborhood for an exotic reason. This killer is reckless and is soon caught.

The Stanos and Bundys are typical of organized killers. They can go from county to county, state to state, leaving a trail of bodies with their special touch on the murder. Authorities never talk to each other to recognize these similarities. Crow explained, "In Stano's case, the bodies were usually laid out similarly. Bra was pulled up above the breast, but not taken off. Pants zipper was pulled down, and small branches would be broken off from trees next to the bodies. Not just shrubbery laid on top of them but small branches.

"Organized killers escalate toward the end," he continued. "Normally they pick people up in the car and take them to a remote location and kill them. When they want to get caught, they go inside. They get desperate. There is a timetable, a body clock. When they go in a building, they give you evidence that you don't normally have. You find a body in the woods or river. What do you have? You find the body in a house and Mother Nature hasn't participated in things. Ted Bundy would never go into a building until Tallahassee. Up to Donna Hensley, Stano never went into a building. Both were effective until they went into a building to kill."

Crow thinks for some reason that Stano had escalated and decided it was time to be caught. For many years—even after being caught—he played very organized mental games about murder.

Thirty

Nearly every woman that Stano murdered had a family and friends who are living victims. Sadly, victims' families have no standing in the law and few legal rights. They often receive poor treatment from government bureaucracies. They must learn to live with their terrible loss while seeking some acknowledgment of that loss by society. They want justice, which translates to revenge or repayment. In many cases there is prolonged trauma, anguish, agony, and, possibly worst of all, personal guilt. In most cases, the victim was first reported missing, then the body was found, but the murderer was unknown. Years later all the grief was renewed when Stano confessed to and eventually was sentenced for these crimes. Each stay of execution intensely fueled the secondary victims' desire to see Stano punished.

Many of the murder victims were from closely knit families. Two were twins with unique twin identification and bonding. Quotes from family members that appeared in the *St. Petersburg Times* when the story broke on December 15, 1982, reflect the intensity of family feelings.

Marine Sgt. Raymond Neal, whose twin sister, Ramona, was murdered by Stano in 1976, asked a reporter where he could write to volunteer to pull the electric chair switch. "I live to see that day, I want to see him fry," said Neal. "You want to meet and torture him. He'll never get his just punishment. He'll never get punishment (enough) for what he has done."

"God, if I got an inch, I'd kill that man," said Albert Bauer, the father of the girl whose body was found in Bradford County. The reporter continued, "Bauer's body tenses, his jaw clenches and his voice is a near-whisper. 'I hate to kill him outright. I want to make him suffer so bad. Christ, you can't imagine. He took something of mine. He owes me. Oh, I might want to share him with some of these other parents, but there is a part of Stano that is mine.' "

Not all victims' relatives want to see Stano executed. Gail Foster's mother does not believe in capital punishment. She said, "It wouldn't bring her back, would it? If he's guilty, I want him to serve his punishment. If he's sick, I think that he should be treated and then serve his punishment."

Many families have kept a communications vigil with the Florida prosecutors on the status of Stano's death cases. Although many live in other states, they call periodically for an update on the prolonged appeal process. In 1985, the State of Florida recognized the suffering of victims and families of victims of crimes and passed a law and constitutional amendment for their fair treatment. A feature of the law requires that homicide victims' families be notified of the arrest, prosecution, sentencing, and appellate review of murderers. Other family and victim assistance such as education, counseling, and cash awards were provided. Over seventy-five per cent of the states now provide victims financial compensation.

Typical of the continuing parental interest and inquiries through the years is Emma Bickrest, mother of Susan Bickrest. She has faithfully called the Attorney General's office to stay informed on the progress of Stano's appeals. Stano was sentenced to death for Susan's murder. When his second death warrant in her case, and his fourth warrant overall, was stayed by the Eleventh Circuit Court of Appeal in May 1988, the Bickrests were called by the media for comments. It had been thirteen years since their daughter's murder.

Mrs. Bickrest said she and her husband have learned to cope with their daughter's death through the help of a support group, Parents of Murdered Children. "But it's always with you your whole life," she said. "Every holiday you miss her.

And to think of that animal there, and they are trying to save his life."

Stano's other two death warrants were for the murder of Cathy Scharf in 1973. Her mother was also contacted concerning Stano's fourth stay of execution. She said that just the thought of Stano provokes her to profanity. "I can't talk nice anymore," she said. "I'm a decent person, but when this comes up I go out of my mind."

The National Organization of Victim Assistance (NOVA) in Washington, D.C., reports that those left behind do in fact face emotional and psychological strain. Often grieving survivors become obsessively preoccupied with the crime. This can result in a wide variety of undesirable symptoms including employment problems, loss of friends, and alienation within the family. Sorrow does not always bring family members closer together, but often works to isolate. Grieving is a lonesome process.

These survivor burdens have caused an increasing number to turn to national organizations like Parents of Murdered Children, with over six thousand members, where they can receive understanding, consolation, and peer group counseling. Another group in Florida dedicated to counseling relatives of murder victims is the League of Victims and Empathizers (LOVE). It has received publicity for vigils outside Florida State Prison urging the execution of Death Row inmates. This, too, is a form of consolation by active participation.

One of the most unusual expressions of survivor outrage was a wrongful death suit for one hundred ten million dollars against Stano, filed by the mother and estate of Mary Carol Maher. They sought ten million to compensate for emotional pain and one hundred million in punitive damages. This successful suit is the highest award in a civil case in United States history. Consider the extension of this case if all survivors filed similar claims. The pain and suffering caused by Stano is almost incalculable. Unfortunately, even survivors who win court judgments cannot collect because Stano has no assets.

In his reflections on the case, Paul Crow always included Stano's parents in the secondary victims. "Those folks got caught up in the frenzy of the press. They really got a raw deal. I've never been able to communicate with them because of the wall built up by the press. I always found Jerry's mother and father to be fine, good, reliable people. When they chose to raise Jerry, nobody had any knowledge about deviate psychological behavior. Certainly not like the knowledge we have today."

When Crow was asked to give seminars on serial killers, concerned parents in the audience had questions about their own children. "How can I tell if Johnny is having a problem?" they asked. Some stated, "I'm worried that my child will be a Bundy, Stano, or Son of Sam." They asked what signs to look for at early stages that would signal cause for concern later.

Crow always responded with graphic examples. "Don't worry about bed-wetting and dumb things around the house. I did dumb things around the house, too," he assured them. "If you have a pet, is it alive and well? Are your neighbor's pets alive and well? If so, no problem. However, if they are fileted in your cellar and your child did it, then you have a problem. This is a first symptom."

He used Ed Kemper of California as an example. "Kemper had an I.Q. of 160. Before he was ten he was cutting the head and limbs off of dolls. Then he did the same thing to small animals. His parents couldn't control him at fifteen and sent him to live with his grandparents. So he killed his parents. He was convicted and jailed, but fooled psychiatrists into letting him out of prison. Before the time of his first parole interview, he had two human heads and four hands in his closet. A creature of habit. His grandmother complained so much that he cut her larynx out and put it down the garbage disposal, cut her head off and put it in the closet. He killed about a dozen women that way."

Bizarre and cruel treatment of dolls and pets at an early age was the warning signal in this instance. Jerry's past had been equally foreboding. Whenever a girl's body was found in the area where the Stanos were living, the family would pick up and move away.

"I can't tell you that Stano's parents were blameless as far as knowing or suspecting what Jerry was doing," Don Jacobson recalled. "I suspect that they did. All I know is that wherever Jerry lived, the bodies were turning up of young women."

The magnitude of Stano's murders can be measured by the huge number of participants, duration and cost of the associated investigations, trials, and appeals.

The investigations were very lengthy for several reasons. Most victims were missing for long periods. Police searched for Barbara Bauer extensively without results. A farmer found her body seven months later. Cathy Scharf was also not found for seven months. It took two years to identify Diana Valleck's remains. Police searched for Phoebe Winston for a year and a half before she was found, and twelve-year-old Susan Basile was never found. Linda Hamilton was found quickly on the beach but could not be identified for many weeks. Two victims have never been identified, and were identified in prosecutions simply as

"Jane Doe." When the body is found later, time eliminates clues. Without identity, investigation is severely hampered. In the Arceneaux and Ligotino murders in Gainesville, police interviewed over two hundred people and spent over five thousand hours looking for clues about the killings without result.

At the time of Stano's killing spree, the criminal justice system was not equipped or trained to deal with serial killers. Paul Crow summarized it, "The killers left many uninvestigated trails and took advantage of the lack of a system. The system did not know how to investigate, interview, cooperate, and prosecute. There was no united front, no central system, no agreement from agency to agency, county to county, state to state."

Police from nine cities and the sheriff's offices from nine counties investigated the Stano murders. FDLE set up and coordinated Task Forces in two areas to assist investigation. Crime laboratories in Sanford and Tallahassee examined Stano's personal possessions and scrutinized the victims' remains. State police from Georgia, Pennsylvania, and New Jersey also investigated murders in their jurisdictions. These investigations totaled tens of thousands of hours and millions of dollars.

The eleven murder convictions required police to document facts of the cases including the confessions and present them in court. All of Stano's lawyers were paid with state funds, with the exception of Don Jacobson. All prosecutors work for the State as do the clerks and judges. Throughout the Stano trials and direct and collateral proceedings to date, over a dozen lawyers have amassed an estimated fifteen thousand hours of time devoted to Stano's case. Add to this the time of eighteen state and federal judges and their clerks and court personnel, and the price of justice for Stano's murders is staggering.

It costs approximately $13,000 a year to house an inmate on Florida's Death Row. Based on a normal life expectancy, life imprisonment for Stano would cost the State just over half a million dollars. The ultimate cost of executing Stano will total over twenty times that cost. What a strange paradox that Stano, such a backward and unaccomplished man, would extract such a ransom from society.

Epilogue

People and places change with time. Daytona's boardwalk area where Stano circled the Loop has vastly improved. Jerry would hardly recognize the area. Groups of civic minded people decided to take back the streets from prostitutes and criminals and began an extensive plan to clean up the area. Meetings were held, long-term plans were made, and wrecking crews were put to work clearing neglected blocks. Buildings were freshly painted and Main Street was resurfaced in attractive brick. Slowly, the tarnished old image took on a new shine.

In the first newly cleared blocks off Atlantic Avenue, a huge, state-of-the-art civic center was built. It attracted new and different crowds to attend quality entertainment. The London Symphony Orchestra plays at the Ocean Center when they are in town. The Ocean Center also attracts big-name groups to suit anyone's musical taste, from Alabama to Michael Bolton to the Moody Blues to Whitney Houston.

Hookers were chased off the streets around the

bandshell, and many of the run-down hotels and apartment buildings that they occupied have been demolished. Some of the buildings were refurbished. The coquina shell wall surrounding the bandshell and the old clock tower, Daytona Beach landmarks for decades, remain intact. But the area around these familiar landmarks is completely modern and rebuilt.

In the bull's-eye of the Loop and directly across from the Ocean Center, a sixteen-floor, worldclass Marriot Hotel appeared in tropical colors of pink, tan, and green. Designed in a pyramid-style, its unique architecture suggests a giant sand castle. Its sprawling arms cover classy shops and trendy restaurants. Between its marble-tiled lobby and the ocean, a sparkling pool reflects handsomely landscaped leisure areas where vacationing families stroll once again. The hotel's expensive interior appointments of brass, glass, and tile spill out toward the ocean walkways and porticos, which lead to additional boutiques and open eating places along the boardwalk.

The Marriot has changed the face of the area and returned the quality and beauty to the beachside, but its position has blocked the infamous Loop. No longer could Stano circle like a shark in search of prey. The traffic pattern is diverted and more manageable. The entire area is safe, inviting, and beautiful.

What has happened to the players in this drama? Many continue in the same roles. Judge Foxman is still a respected Circuit Court Judge in Daytona Beach. Judge Fawcett remains on the United States District Court in Orlando. Judge Goshorn has been elevated from the Circuit Court in Brevard County to the Florida Fifth District Court of Appeals. The first prosecutor, Larry Nixon, left the State Attorney's Office and now has a successful private practice in Daytona Beach. Prosecutor Dean Moxley was appointed to a Circuit Court Judge position in Brevard County. Assistant Attorney General Margene Roper continues to prosecute Stano's capital appeals as the Chief of the Capital Division in the Daytona Beach Office. Assistant Attorney General Belle Turner first entered the case as a legal intern assisting Prosecutor Nixon in the Bickrest and Muldoon sentencing in 1983. She later joined the Attorney General's Office the following year and represented the State in Stano's direct and collateral appeals, and continues to work there today as the Bureau Chief.

Howard Pearl remains one of three specialists in the Public Defender's Office who defends persons accused of capital crimes. Don Jacobson left private practice and joined Pearl in the Public Defender's Office. The other lawyers that represented Stano, Russo and Quarles, remain in the Public Defender's Office as well. Friedland is in private practice in Titusville. He unsuccessfully ran for judge in 1992. Mark Olive has left the Florida Capital Collateral Representative's Office and works for Florida State University, but he continues to represent Stano today in his final appeals in federal court.

Paul Crow had a meteoric rise in the Daytona Beach Police Department. In addition to being selected National Police Officer of the Month in connection with the Stano case, he solved a series of notable cases. He was promoted from Sergeant to Captain to Chief of Police in a short time.

Gerald Stano remains on Death Row in Florida State Prison. He has seen all Florida courts reject his appeals. He knows that the review of his case in federal court is drawing to a close. Ted Bundy was executed on his fourth death warrant in January 1989. Stano has survived four death warrants already. Once he got within three hours of his scheduled execution, and even ate his last meal. Soon the federal courts will decide the pending Stano cases. This pressure has triggered several strokes. Stano still has a sense of humor. He recently wrote letters saying that his attorneys are trying to get him killed. Eventually, a fifth death warrant will be signed by the governor and will be enforced.

Stano knows this and waits.